MUSIC
THROUGH
THE EYES OF
FAITH

MUSIC THROUGH THE EYES OF FAITH

Harold M. Best

Christian College Coalition
For Enduring Values

■ HarperSanFrancisco
A Division of HarperCollins*Publishers*

The Christian College Coalition is an association of Christian liberal arts colleges and universities across North America. More than thirty Christian denominations, committed to a variety of theological traditions and perspectives, are represented by our member colleges. The views expressed in this volume are primarily those of the authors and are not intended to serve as a position statement of the Coalition membership. For more information about the Christian College Coalition write to: Christian College Coalition, 329 Eighth Street, NE, Washington, DC 20002.

Library of Congress Cataloging-in-Publication Data

Best, Harold M.
    Music through the eyes of faith / Harold M. Best. — 1st ed.
       p.   cm.
    Includes bibliographical references.
    ISBN 0-06-060862-5 (acid-free paper)
      1. Music—Religious aspects—Christianity.   2. Music—Philosophy and aesthetics.   I. Title.
    ML3871.B47   1993   92-53911
    246'.7—dc20   CIP

93 94 95 96 97 CWI 10 9 8 7 6 5 4 3 2 1

This edition is printed on acid-free paper that meets the American National Standards Institute Z39.48 Standard.

MUSIC TASK FORCE MEMBERS

Anton Armstrong
St. Olaf College

Karen DeMol
Dordt College

Charlotte Kroeker
Whitworth College

Ken Medema
Brier Patch Music

Richard Stanislaw
King College

Paul Westermeyer
Luther Northwestern Theological Seminary

John Worst
Calvin College

SERIES ADVISORY BOARD MEMBERS

Nicholas Wolterstorff
Yale University

David Benner
Redeemer College

Richard Bube
Richard University

David Allen Hubbard
Fuller Theological Seminary

Karen Longman
Christian College Coalition

Ann Paton
Geneva College

Timothy Smith
Johns Hopkins University

Richard T. Wright
Gordon College

Pied Beauty

Glory be to God for dappled things—
For skies of couple-colour as a brinded cow;
For rose-moles all in a stipple upon trout that swim;
Fresh-firecoal chestnut-falls; finches' wings;
Landscape plotted and pieced—fold, fallow, and plough;
And all trades, their gear and tackle and trim.

All things counter, original, spare, strange;
Whatever is fickle, freckled (who knows how?)
With swift, slow; sweet, sour; adazzle, dim;
He fathers-forth whose beauty is past change:
Praise him.

—Gerard Manley Hopkins

Any tone can succeed any other tone, any tone can
sound simultaneously with any other tone or tones,
and any group of tones can be followed by any other
group of tones, just as any degree of tension or
nuance can occur in any medium under any kind of
stress or duration. Successful projection will depend
upon the contextual and formal conditions that
prevail, and upon the skill and the soul of the
composer.

—Vincent Persichetti

CONTENTS

FOREWORD

This is a remarkable book. I can best communicate what is remarkable about it by simply quoting a few words from the introduction. The author, Harold M. Best, a professor of music widely known and honored in his profession, has just been talking autobiographically about the ways in which, for most of his life, his love for music of a wide variety of different sorts made for tension in his life. People around him and his own inner voice told him that most of what he liked was bad; commitment to quality in music requires the rejection of musical pluralism. He then says this:

. . . in these later years of my profession, I find myself laughing and whole again, musically happier than ever, celebrating this vast expanse of sonic creativity, longing with all my heart to be a world musician as a living part of being a world Christian, and delighting in teaching all of this renewed good news. I find myself wanting to dance through a Pentecost of musics, excited as never before, rejecting older, narrower, restrictive canons, continuing to embrace the musics they exclusively praised, while rejoining other musics I had for too long turned my back on. . . . Yet there is a significant amount of music that I simply cannot bring myself to enjoy, because even though I revel in diversity, I strive for personal excellence. In other words, I still make choices, and I truly believe that there is music of poor quality—far too much of it—right alongside the good music.

Those words give clear hints of what is remarkable in this book: A vivid style; a deep and wide knowledge of the field of music combined with a love of performance, an insistence on the importance of excellence combined with an extraordinary breadth of musical taste and a courageous celebration of humanity's music in all its diversity; a deep and unashamed piety combined with theological sophistication.

What Harold Best sees when he looks at music through the eyes of his deeply felt, reflective, and generous Christian faith is an extraordinarily rich and exciting panorama. He tackles the tough questions that come to mind when people of faith reflect on music; when he's not entirely satisfied with the answers he proposes, he tells us so. He strives for wholeness, integrity, between his life of faith and his life in music. But I predict that what will stay with the reader of this book longer than the memory of intellectual stimulation and longer than the memory of religious seriousness is the memory of celebration: a person of faith and learning celebrating great music in all its diversity.

Nicholas Wolterstorff
Yale University

ACKNOWLEDGMENTS

While books are written for the benefit of communities, communities are necessary to the writing of books. To three communities in particular I owe my gratitude for their help in bringing this book about.

The first is a group of people who have been directly connected to the writing project itself: Karen Longman, vice president of the Christian College Coalition, along with the members of the project task force: Nicholas Wolterstorff, Anton Armstrong, Karen DeMol, Charlotte Kroeker, Ken Medema (and Beverly VanderMolen, who read every word of the book to Ken while Ken dictated his responses on cassette), Richard Stanislaw, Paul Westermeyer, and John Worst. Each of these good people spent many hours giving preliminary advice, planning a very successful national conference, reading the manuscript, and artfully combining critique with support. Once a passable first draft was completed, Beth Weber at Harper San Francisco led me carefully and candidly through rewrites, which not only improved the original but also taught me much about becoming a better writer. Without generous funding from the Murdoch Trust, it would be difficult to see how the national conference or the book would have been so easily expedited.

The second community is that of higher education and its scholarship, particularly the Christian part of it. I remember the first time, some thirty years ago, when I first heard the words "Christian worldview" and "the integration of faith and learning." I remember the intellectual freshening that broke in on me then as

I began to understand how powerfully unifying God's truth is. This freshening continues to this day, thanks to the colleagues who grace the laboratories of Christian thought. Many of these colleagues are well known and widely read. Others are not. But beyond the books and lectureships, the richer joy of the community of higher education lies in an ongoing collective wisdom that, in the highest sense, is "public domain," uncopyrighted. This kind of wisdom is shared around cups of coffee, brown bag lunches; it is overheard in a lecture, debated a few minutes here and there, tucked away in a term paper, picked up in prayer meetings and Christmas parties. It nurtures gently, unpretentiously, and gradually, the way legumes, whole-grain bread, and hearty porridges do.

The third community is that of my family—my wife, children, and grandchildren. This is the community where faith and living—gently, familially, and lovingly—anoint the rigors of faith and learning. I have no adequate way of showing my thanksgiving for these nearby images of God except to dedicate this book to them, to endeavor to love them all the more, and to ask you, the reader, to rejoice in your loved ones and to live the Christian life to the fullest in their presence.

Harold M. Best

INTRODUCTION

Unless you . . . become like little children . . .

—MATT. 18:3 (NIV)

When I became a man, I did away with childish things.

—1 COR. 13:11 (NASB)

Let all the world in every corner sing:
My God and King!

—GEORGE HERBERT

I ask that you allow me to begin personally, partly to show that, even though I am a professional musician, my musical background was quite ordinary. It contained no spectacular people, no extraordinary mechanisms, no mystical events. It was just a part of growing up: a musical world indivisibly joined to a larger world. Give or take a few shifts of age and culture, it was a world not unlike yours, rooted in the everyday, the personal, and the real. And because things did not always go musically right for me; because there were real problems and eventual solutions, it might help if I let you in on them.

My father, a minister of the gospel, and my mother, a gentle, lovely woman, were amateur musicians whose childhood was likewise graced by amateur musicians. My father's mother sang alto in a Lutheran church choir, and my mother's father played the cornet in the local municipal band. My mother played the piano and my father was a more-than-decent violinist, largely self-taught. They played in church and for friends, but mostly for each other. Hearing them make music together and singing to me were among my earliest musical memories.

I remember an upright piano in our living room on which I made the plinking and plunking music of little children. I remember a few violin lessons from my father—breaking my arm thankfully brought them to a close—and then my first piano lessons from my mother. In second grade in a small public school in Sharon, Pennsylvania, I learned how *do*, *re*, *mi* could be used to help me sing tunes. I also discovered that I could turn what I heard back into *do*, *re*, and *mi*. Sometime before I could read music very well, I was trying to make it up. I didn't know that this was called improvisation—I just thought that this was one of the things you did with music. My next piano teacher—an itinerant pedagogue, seventy-five cents a lesson, portly and straddle-legged beside me on the bench, awash in recent cigar smoke—was the first of several teachers, as our family moved from one pastorate to another.

At home the music we listened to was classical music. My father did not find popular music acceptable. Even when I was an adult professional and he a senior citizen, he remained puzzled and uncomfortable over my enthusiasm for the many kinds of popular music that I had eagerly come to embrace. His love for Bach and Brahms and Beethoven and all organ music was so intense, so natural and unschooled, that I grew up assuming that this was a common part of common living. To this day, I remain deeply grateful for his values, exclusive as they were.

But still I got wind of popular music, on the radio and from my friends: semiclassical, popular ballads, the emerging style of boogie-woogie, and swing. I fell in love with this music, not even guessing that it could be separated out from Bach and Brahms and Beethoven. I also heard what we now call ethnic music, without any idea that it could be separated out into classes and hierarchies. I simply knew that I needed all of these kinds of music as much as I needed the classical music that my father had personally singled out. To me, it was all one enchanting world, each part merging with the rest.

Enchanting, that is, until I began to hear that all of this popular stuff wasn't spiritual—that it was the music of the world, therefore of worldliness. Thus my one world of music became divided, not aesthetically but spiritually, into "good" music and "bad" music. The music I heard in church was, of course, "good" music, but even within this world a significant split occurred. Sunday morning music turned out to be different than Sunday evening music. Sunday morning and its music was for tried-and-true Christians. It was connected to worship and topical Christianity. Sunday evening was for those who needed the Lord. Beginning in a "song service," its music was almost inevitably linked to promptings, warnings, sadness for sins, and repentance. These two Sunday musics were basically in the same styles. The difference, as I now look back on it, lay in the contexts. While you may not be able to identify with this morning-evening experience, I would imagine that you have experienced some kind of split in your musical experience. And this, it turns out, is a crucial matter for people everywhere.

The split between "good" and "bad" music—with precious little middle ground—also occurred in my academic training. There was one kind of good music: the music of the great masters. John Thompson's red piano books and newly minted sheet music pressed me forward from problem to problem and composer to composer. This was the music that, though I had no inkling at the time, was beginning to train me for the academic and philosophical world of college degrees and professional music making. And there were two kinds of bad music: low-quality classical music and almost everything else—popular, jazz, gospel, country, and so on. For far too long, I lived openly in the sophisticated world of the classics and privately in the musics of the "other side," not fully knowing myself anymore, not so sure that what I had once so naturally embraced was to be trusted. I began to wonder if I was a musical hybrid or hypocrite, publicly and pedagogically touting the party line while inwardly drawn to so much more.

But despite many years of disintegrative musical training, clean through a doctorate, and a considerable way into a professional career; despite my place within the ranks of the musical idolaters and ridiculers; and thanks to a spiritual brokenness that reintroduced me to the fullness of Christ and the principled wonder of the Scriptures, I began to put these worlds back together and to re-enter once more the delights of early childhood, revisiting and celebrating one world of music, by now larger and grander than ever.

And in these later years of my profession, I find myself laughing and whole again, musically happier than ever, celebrating this vast expanse of sonic creativity, longing with all my heart to be a world musician as a living part of being a world Christian, and delighting in teaching all of this renewed good news. I find myself wanting to dance through a Pentecost of musics, excited as never before, rejecting older, narrower, restrictive canons, but continuing to embrace the musics they exclusively praised, while rejoining other musics I had for too long turned my back on. And, thanks to the world of ethnomusicology, I discover—almost daily—new sounds, new textures, new reasons, new combinations, along with deeper and wider aesthetic values.

My record, tape, and CD library is full of all kinds of music from Renaissance to twentieth century; from rock to jazz to country; from the music of the eastern highlands of Papua New Guinea to Appalachian folk, to Delta blues and gospel. I love classic twelve-bar blues, and I practice them regularly; or if I'm lucky enough to sit in with a jazz group, I try my hand at the exhilarating experience of group improvisation. Above and around all of this, Johann Sebastian Bach is still my best friend and, right next to him, a wild assortment of music and music makers: Béla Bartók, Paul Desmond, Max Roach, Igor Stravinsky, Erroll Garner, Keith Jarrett, Chet Baker, Brahms, Poulenc, bluegrass, the Uptown String Quartet, Doctor John, Junior Wells, Stevie Ray Vaughan (thanks to my youngest son), zydeco, Milt Jackson, Mozart, Take Six, Prokofiev, and numberless anonymous folk, tribal, ethnic, and back-porch music makers. And always near my heart and lips are "Jesus Loves Me," "Amazing Grace," "Yesterday," "Georgia on My Mind," and "Mister Bojangles."

Yet there is a significant amount of music that I simply cannot bring myself to enjoy, because even though I revel in diversity, I strive for personal excellence. In other words, I still make choices, and I truly believe that there is music of poor quality—far too much of it—right alongside the good music. The beauty of all of this is that excellence and diversity are compatible. And for those who own Jesus, a thousand musical tongues will never be enough to praise him.

Everybody has a personal world of music; mine is just one. In Papua New Guinea, tribal musicians get their songs in their dreams. These are joined to the songs of their ancestors and constitute the communal song of the entire tribe. They unify past and present, memory and immediate reality. Music and life are of one cloth.

Within the boundaries of our own culture is a world quite similar to the one of tribal musicians, where people make wonderful music without benefit of formal academic training. Many of them can't read music. Their minds, fingers, and chops have picked up amazing things with no other teaching except that of hearing, imitating, and making up the next new lick. They have learned to "think" in music without benefit of a preexisting knowledge "about" music. They improvise, experiment, experience, listen, copy, and create.

And in a time when too many are trying to ignore or condemn it, there is the wonderful and remarkable world of classical music. It is immensely rich and variegated; it plumbs the depths of intellect and spirit in ways that many other kinds of music have little time for. This classical world—not all of it, but the very best of it—has consistently shown that quality and integrity are to be sought out at any cost. And its best practitioners, along with their colleagues in other kinds of music, have come to understand that one kind of good music reaches out into the goodness of other kinds.

And for the worshiping Christian, there are masses, motets, chant, gospel songs, hymns, chorales, Scripture songs, cantatas, praise choruses, Christian contemporary, anthems, and Sunday school songs.

Then there is the world of children's music, world round; the music of rope skipping, circling and jumping, dancing and fantasy.

It is the world of making things up, of direct, active, spontaneous song; a world in which circumstance, movement, gesture, and pitch are not all that easily separated. This is a world knit to games, pretending, stories, sleeping and waking up, loving a doll, taunting, and cajoling. It is also a world that is gradually formalized by music lessons, Sunday school, the rituals of the media: cartoons, Mister Rogers, Sesame Street and commercials, and eventually MTV. And it all too often becomes a world of increasing peer pressure and media manipulation, a world of incipient narrowness in which the capability for loving all musics may gradually be numbed and provincialized.

And how would we make music without the genius of the instrument makers: from Bali to India to Cremona, from Appalachia to Scotland, and into the most remote societies of Africa and the South Pacific? This is a world of leather, wood, metal, catgut, fulcrums, feathers, reeds, electrical circuitry, bamboo, pernambuco, plectra, keyboards, mallets, rosin, varnish, tweeters, woofers, valves, sequencers, acoustical law, and human imagination. From a simple mouth harp to a gigantic pipe organ; from a one-string Ugandan *enzenze* to a fully equipped electronic studio, we have a gigantic world of color at our disposal.

As long as there are people there will be music. The world they live in is a startlingly lovely, confusing, and warring place, and the music they make springs out of every conceivable circumstance, from political protest to childbirth to military conflict. This musical world is made up of teachers, students, critics, shamans, geniuses, dreamers, and hucksters. It is a world of commerce, idolatry, servanthood and ministry, manipulation and holy moment. It is a world of unity, divisiveness, appropriateness, wisdom, elegance, heresy, crassness, craftsmanship, greed, and altruism. This is a world in which people have, in countless ways, celebrated their existence in sound, searching for something for which, in the words of Ken Medema, "There is no other way of saying it."

But music does not exist all by itself. Along with all the sound, color, rhythm, texture, shape, and celebration, many issues demand probing and resolution: issues of content and context, faith and practice, relativity and exactitude, splits and unities, ethics, truth, and excellence.

All Christians, inside and outside of music, have the same task: they must live and work, decide and do, with the mind of Christ. This is more than having facts about Christ, learning Scripture, entering into salvation, or seeing Christianity as a kind of sanctified braininess. It is a way of living of such magnitude that, as the apostle Paul says, we are actually enabled to test and approve what God's good, pleasing, and perfect will is (Romans 12:2), equipping us for every good work (2 Timothy 3:17). This kind of integration is not an event but a process. As hard as we might try, the final integrative model will never quite appear. And sometimes it is almost impossible to know what is right and what isn't. This is why we must continually seek out and drink in the truth, wrestling with it, being stumped by it, yet faithfully trusting it, even when the smoky glass comes in between and calls things into question that should be as clear as noonday. The temptation will come to turn from deciding and doing to debating about deciding and doing, and integration can become an exercise in speculation instead of a way of life. Furthermore, we can make the mistake of integrating our faith into our learning, instead of the reverse. Or we can create emulsions, which look like integrations as long as we keep everything agitated and busied up. But once we set them aside and let them settle out, the layers reappear and we, or perhaps others, see them for what they really are: dualism, spiritualized secularism, or bald hypocrisy.

In writing *Music Through the Eyes of Faith*, I have tried to keep two purposes before me at all times: to celebrate the uniqueness of music making as part of the larger world of human creativity, and to hold that music making is subordinate to, and informed by, the larger doctrines of creation, worship, offering, faith, grace, stewardship, redemptive witness, excelling, and love.

This approach implies that music *per se* will not always be directly discussed—it is both subject and object. Time will be spent outlining the essence of biblical paradigms of which music making is, for the Christian, a symptom, not a cause. This strategy is based on the idea that, just as God's creation or handiwork—in all of its stunning variety—is less than God and in submission to God's purposes, so human creativity, of which music is but one part, is in submission both to God and to its human makers. This approach allows for music both to be celebrated and kept in its place.

Deriving out of the foregoing, I make a defense for musical pluralism, one of the book's central themes. However, my discussion of pluralism is not based on current cultural and academic buzzwords about multiculturalism, the downgrading of Western culture, and the politicization of human creativity. Instead, it flows directly out of timeless truths that have always been nearby but not always plumbed for their deeper meaning.

Once pluralism is established and defended, I take up issues of personal excellence and musical quality, in light of the following: (1) Music is part of a divinely ordained world of relativism. (2) This particular relativism (in no way to be confused with moral relativism) stands in stark contrast, and complete subjection to, the absoluteness of truth. (3) A biblically and sociologically healthy musical pluralism depends on having a center—a musical and cultural home—from and to which all musical sojourning takes place. This kind of centeredness is readily distinguished from prejudice or superiority. (4) Musical pluralism is not complete without classical music. This goes contrary to the current idea that multiculturalism not only disassociates itself from but also protests against classical Western culture. It is further contrary to the idea that multiculturalism is limited to a few selected ethnic and popular musics, namely those of Hispanic and African American origins.

While *Music Through the Eyes of Faith* is not intended to be iconoclastic, it does call some traditional assumptions into question: (1) The traditional coupling of truth and beauty is argued to be artificial and less than biblical. A new paradigm is argued for, based on revelation and creation, or truth and handiwork. (2) Neither entertainment nor immediate gratification is considered wrong or even questionable, unless either one turns out to exclude all other modes of perception. (3) Music and worship are disconnected as to cause and effect. Music is neither an aid to worship nor a tool for producing it. It is an offering, uniquely given over to God, who is both means and end. (4) While the question of musical quality cannot be overlooked in the face of pluralism, it must be addressed in a different light because of pluralism. Just as there is no universal music, there is no universal aesthetic. The trick lies in locating and defining quality amidst the plethora of legitimate musics. Admittedly, this was the most difficult section of the book for me to write.

I have tried, in all cases, to make the book readable, but I assume that Christians really like to think, as long as there is something worth thinking about. I say this because, in the many years I have spent with pastors, ministers of music, laypersons, seminary students, and undergraduates, I have never lost faith in the ability of stewardly and dedicated people to value ideas and to work hard at thinking things through. I remain firmly convinced of this, despite those who shrink back from challenging hungry minds and engage in trendy talk about "meeting them where they are" and "meeting their felt needs."

Above all, I want my readers to know three things: (1) I love them, whoever they are. (2) I want to join and help them in their love of, and quest for, the best possible music. (3) Neither they nor I can afford to shirk the awesome task of separating out the musical wheat from the chaff, no matter the cost. However I may fail or err, I hope and pray that this effort will turn out to point toward wisdom, usefulness, and, above all, scriptural soundness.

Chapter 1

GOD'S CREATION, HUMAN CREATIVITY, AND MUSIC MAKING

Creation seems to be delegation through and through. He will do nothing simply of Himself which can be done by creatures. I suppose this is because He is a giver. And he has nothing to give but Himself. And to give Himself is to do His deeds—in a sense, and on varying levels to be Himself—through the things he has made.

—C. S. LEWIS

Where were you when I laid the foundations of the earth! . . . and all the sons of God shouted for joy? Have you ever in your life commanded the morning . . . Have you entered the springs of the sea? Where is the way to the dwelling of the light?

—GOD TO JOB, JOB 38:4–19 (NASB)

[The sounds of nature] are promises of music; it takes a human being to keep them.

—IGOR STRAVINSKY

Music doesn't just happen; it has to be made, worked out. Sometimes this working out is spontaneous, other times greatly labored and time consuming. But, in any case, questions like these come to mind: Why can we make music and how do so many people go about making it in so many ways? Is making music like making other things? What is creativity itself? Where does creativity come from?

Creativity is not just for artists and music makers, it is a part of our humanity. Everybody, to one degree or another, is creative. Therefore a simple definition of the term is important. *Creativity is the ability to imagine something—think it up—and then execute it or make it.* [1] In the case of music, a music maker will imagine, work out, or dream up a piece of music that can then be presented. This combination of thinking up and presenting can take place in two ways. The music maker can think up the music in advance and then present it, either from memory or from some kind of a written code. Or the music can be thought up and presented simultaneously. In the first case, we think primarily of a performed composition and in the second, an improvisation. In either case, coming up with the music and then presenting it represents a union of imagining and crafting.

The quality of the crafting will be determined by the degree of technique and skill the maker possesses. Technique and skill are closely connected: technique is the facilitator and skill is the degree and refinement of the facility. As imagination increases and technique and skill become more sophisticated, there will be a corresponding increase of uniqueness, subtlety, and finesse. This is as true of the creation of a super computer as it is of a work of art. Yet creativity, technique, and skill often get mixed up with each other in the musical world. The making of music does not always signal the presence of creativity. If I am creative, I imagine a different way of music making than someone else would. I must then possess the skill to execute this difference. If I can only duplicate someone else's music making, I am not creative but merely skillful. If my imitation of someone else is third-rate, then neither skill nor creativity is apparent.

As astonishing as human creativity is, it cannot satisfactorily explain itself. Philosophical and psychological attempts to explain creativity are useful but only carry us so far. To understand further, we must pursue the connection among Creator, creation, creature, and creativity. Then we can better understand why we are the way we are and why we possess this uncanny knack of coming up with things that have not been around before.

We have two primary sources to guide us: the Scriptures and the creation. Between the truth of the Scriptures—the maker's Word—and the testimony of the creation—the maker's work—we are provided with the clearest principles for guiding our creativity. God is both the supreme imaginer and the consummate craftsman, the true poet and the exacting grammarian. What God richly imagines God also carefully structures. And with undeniable clarity, the whole creation at once proclaims its maker and serves as the best possible model we can ever have for our own creativity.

What do the creator and the creation show us then? How can God's way of making things show us more about our creativity and how we can be its best stewards? There are several concepts which we need to study.

God's Names and Creatorhood, and Human Creativity

Some of the most direct references to God's creatorhood lie outside the Genesis accounts, in the Psalms, the prophetic books, and the all-important passages in Colossians (1:15–17) and Hebrews (1:3). In the Colossians passage, Christ is named as the one in whom all created things continue to hold together. The Hebrews passage speaks of the direct and ongoing relationship of the triune God to his creation. We are told that for as long as the creation holds together and keeps on working it does so only because the Word of the power of Christ decides that it is so. In other words, God is not a disinterested maker. God is directly and continually engaged with his handiwork. Natural laws continue to work because Christ is now saying so; the galaxies continue to speed away from each other because Christ is now saying so; we continue to live, move, and have our being because Christ is now saying so.

As important as the Colossians and Hebrews passages are, another passage takes us more to the heart of the subject. The account of Moses and the burning bush (Exodus 3:1–14) articulates a dimension that is foundational to any other concept of God.[2] Moses was the first person in recorded Scripture to ask God specifically, "Who are you?" The response was brief and direct: "I AM THAT I AM" (verse 14). In as clear a way as words make possible, God declared Himself to be absolutely noncontingent, self-inhering, and self-sufficient. The middle word, *that*, is crucial: the name would be flawed without it. God is God—he is that he is. Nothing started him up. Nothing can be added as to how or why he exists. God is eternally and changelessly complete being God. There is no growing up into, no need for improvement. God has no need to look back and wonder if there is another way to be God.

But despite the foundational completeness of this name, it is not God's whole name. Throughout Scripture, God is given a vast assortment of other names, each referring either to his being (I AM THAT I AM) or doing. If we were to collect all the names that refer to God's doing, we would come up with a name similar to the I AM name: I ACT THAT I ACT. God's doing is noncontingent, self-inhering, infinitely sovereign, and whole. All that God does is of his self-sufficiency, for his own reasons, and without flaw. In the words of the psalmist, God is good and what He does, is good (Psalm 119:68).

However, God is not a divided God. Being and doing are not cause and effect but aspects of each other. God did not need to create in order to prove anything, to become authentic or credible or to satisfy an unmet need. God is not I AM BECAUSE I ACT or I WILL BECOME IF I DO ENOUGH or any such combination. Rather, God sovereignly chose to imagine and make the creation, not because he had to but because he wanted to. Consequently, the creation is simply a satisfaction of choice. Had God not made the creation, God would still be the Creator, self-caused, entirely complete. In a way that eludes us, the triune God can be eternally at work within himself, disclosing the fullness of himself to himself and infinitely rich within these disclosures.

What does this mean to our creativity and music making? Above all, it means that we should not make music in order to prove that we are or to authenticate ourselves. God created in us the capability for understanding that we are authenticated in him, not in what we do. While we, as created beings, are entirely dependent and contingent, we are to image forth in our being and doing all that God is and does. God's character and attributes—holiness, love, mercy, wisdom, creatorhood, power, graciousness, and justice—are to be our character and attributes, exercised and expressed through our finitude, in complete dependence on and harmony with God. The Christian gospel is a message of becoming a new creation, whereby we are returned to the glory and dignity of dependence and worship and to the reunification of being and doing. In light of this, the union of being and doing becomes a perpetual offering, an act of continued worship (Romans 12:1).

In the final analysis, music making is neither a means nor an end but an offering, therefore an act of worship. All music makers everywhere must understand this and proceed accordingly. Nothing but harm lies ahead if we try to authenticate ourselves with our musical works or become so attached to them—*addicted* might be a better word—that we have no sense of worth or being without this "proof" of our existence. To repeat something said earlier, our union with God, both in our createdness and our redemption, is the only authenticity worth claiming. And our music making must continually bear witness to that.

The Creator Is Not the Creation and the Music Maker Is Not the Music

Some religious systems equate their gods with nature. Others believe that parts of nature are inhabited or animated by spirits and are, consequently, to be avoided, worshiped, feared, or adored. Still other religious systems modify these approaches by maintaining that a being quite similar to the Judeo-Christian God "is" everything that has been made. While orthodox Christians can say that God is everywhere, as much in the middle of an oak tree as in the space around it, they do not say that God is an oak tree or is one with it.

In other words, while it is entirely true that God created— thought up and executed—the first oak tree, God is not an oak tree, nor is the oak tree all the more special because it participates in God's being. Likewise, while it is true that God cherishes everything made and calls it good, it is not true that God is attached to creation the way a parent is to his or her child. Nor is God bound to creation in the same way as to the only begotten Son or, for that matter, to us.[3] As glorious as the creation is, it was merely created and not begotten. A strawberry, a galaxy, a dolphin, and a sea lion are not in the image of God. They are handiwork, pure and simple, thus of an entirely different order.

This next point is crucial. Having made the creation and having created us in his image, God has given us a particular assignment that could not have been given to any other created beings. In telling Adam and Eve to rule over the fish of the sea and the birds of the air and over every living creature that moves on the ground (Genesis 1:28), God was setting down a basic principle. Man and woman, created in the image of God, possessed of enormous creative powers, made capable of love, wisdom, holiness, justice, and the like, are neither the same as the rest of the creation nor subject to it. While materially they can be outweighed by a mountain or overpowered by the force of the ocean, and while they are incapable of changing the speed of light, they cannot be morally, spiritually, or behaviorally overcome by anything in the creation around them.

These concepts are extremely important to the Christian music maker, especially when there are so many artists who are mastered by what they do and believe themselves to be incarnate in it. A Christian musician has every right to cherish what he or she has made and to call it good. And all of us have every right to be concerned when we see people despising or misusing each other's musical works—even those that may not be as good as others. But the matter stops there. We must remember that, just as we were created to hold dominion over the creation, we are to be in dominion over our music. And just as God is not the creation, so we are not our music.

As artists and music makers, we must overcome the temptation to make art and music so large, so other, so mystical, that they become more than us, wielding certain powers that they were never intended to have and given more value than they could ever intrinsically possess. Biblical ways of making music are rooted in a humbled and realistic sense of human work and creativity. Whenever musicians acknowledge the link between creativity and craftsmanship, and when the nobility of being made in the image of God is coupled to the humble and ordinary stuff of work, servanthood, and community, we come much closer to the truth. Music makers of other times and deeper beliefs are worth remembering. Johann Sebastian Bach and generations of church musicians immediately before and after him considered themselves to be simple craftsmen, given a job to do, doing it carefully, usefully, and humbly and, most of all, for the glory of God.

While there is absolutely nothing inherently wrong with being famous or being a star, there is a danger in making things out of stardom and fame that simply should not be made—things that impede the quiet, humble flow of homespun and temperate creativity. Many Christian music makers give the impression of being dissatisfied with anything less than major, outsized productions, as if "bigger is better" were somehow authored by God—as if these were the only ways God could be enticed to drop from the skies and "minister" to his people or move an unregenerate soul closer to the Kingdom.

The Fall, Creativity, and Music Making

Whenever Christians think about creativity and music making, we are bound to wonder how the Fall affects and infects what we do. Perhaps we should ask this question instead: As horrible as the Fall is, do we make too much of it by trying to guess what it is all by itself, instead of talking about how God works within it and helps us overcome it, even while we continue to sin?

There are two things we can agree on: Nobody really knows what it was like before the Fall, and nobody knows what it is like to be unfallen. The accounts in the first few chapters of Genesis contain no direct information about the circumstances, conditions, and routines of the unfallen world. There is no information about how long the creation remained unfallen or how long Adam and Eve were able to enjoy the world in which they were placed. We have no idea of the things they did, how they were at work uniting with, subduing, and overseeing God's handiwork. And there is no information about what we call music, architecture, or technology; nor is there a clue as to how what we call artistic change or technological shifts might have come about in the context of perfection and harmony. We can only surmise that things were not static, that Adam and Eve were somehow at work, not so much in making things better (the way we think of better), but actively caring for and creatively using the creation, probing the mysteries of their own personal uniqueness, and doing a kind of work that can only be described as moving from perfection to perfection. If there was music—and all music makers would naturally want to assume that there must have been—what did it sound like? Did the overtone series have a different configuration than it does now? Or did God leave it alone, along with other certain natural laws, even after the Fall? These and countless other questions come to mind, all because we know something to be quite wrong and we look for something better. And part of our wrongness is shown in our dissatisfaction with what we have, even though it might possess remarkable beauty and integrity. Between the dissatisfaction and the beauty our creativity continues to search for, and proclaim, better ways.

But instead of getting into useless speculation about what unfallen music is like or what the Fall actually did to music and whether becoming a Christian can in any way fix the music up, let's concentrate on something that almost never comes to mind: the music that Jesus heard and made throughout his life—the music of the wedding feast, the dance, the street, and the synagogue. As it turns out, Jesus was not a composer but a carpenter. Thus he heard and used the music made by other, fallen creatures—the very ones he died to redeem.

The ramifications of this single fact are enormous. They assist in answering the questions as to whether music used by Christians can only be written by Christians and whether music written by non-

Christians is somehow non-Christian. But for now, it is important to understand that even though we don't know whether every piece of music Jesus used was written by people of faith, we can be sure that it was written by imperfect people, bound by the conditions of a fallen world and hampered by sinfulness and limitation. So even though we do not know what musical perfection is, we do know that the perfect one could sing imperfect music created by fallen and imperfect people, while doing so completely to the glory of his heavenly Father. And we also know that unredeemed people make incredibly beautiful music, that redeemed people can make some inferior music, and that the history of musical creativity is one of interchange among people—Christians and Christians as well as Christians and non-Christians.

In short, the making of beautiful music is not the sole prerogative of redeemed people while the making of ugly music is left to the wicked. As much as some Christians try to make this out to be the case, it simply does not work that way. Rather, we must understand that there is a profound difference between a wicked heart and wicked art (as trite as that may sound). As we shall see in a later chapter, there are biblical reasons for separating who people are from what they make.

The Imagined Creation, Human Imagination, and Music Making

When we think of God creating, we usually focus our attention on an exercise of almighty power in bringing substance out of nothingness.[4] This is an unsettling mystery for us, since we have absolutely no such capability. But there is another mystery, just as perplexing: *God not only brought the creation out of nothing, God thought it up out of nothing.* Without advice, maps, plans, models, or prototypes, the all-knowing creator thought up giraffes, quarks, wind, cucumbers, the overtone series, sexual reproduction, natural law, dolphins, and strawberries. When we limit ourselves to the concept of an already-made creation as the primary model for artistic creativity, we get an incomplete picture of what creativity really is. What we should concentrate on first is what happened when God created the first day, the first time around. This forces us to a fundamental principle about artistic activity, from which additional ones may be derived.

1. *God is the first abstract, nonrepresentational imaginer, because what God first imagined and crafted did not represent or imitate anything. Each thing made was thought up, purely and simply, in and of itself and without prior reference.* A great deal of fuss is made over nonrepresentation in the arts. Through a complex and flawed conceptual evolution, we have been taught that art should imitate, that it should be a picture *of* instead of simply a picture. The result is that art is all too often judged in direct proportion to its ability to be "realistic." If it "looks like," it is more acceptable than if it doesn't. As long as we can see a barn or a daisy or a seascape in a painting we feel secure, because we can refer to the "real" barn, daisy, or seascape for comparison. As a result, artists are often limited to or judged by nothing more than penmanship. The proclivity toward imitation may derive out of flawed worldviews, especially those that hold to an ideal, essentialized reality that the artist is obligated to imitate or copy. Imitation can also issue out of a fear of newness, an addiction to repetition, or the safety of the familiar. Or it could be the result of an even more disturbing reality, namely that of Lucifer's desire to "be like the Most High." In this sense, imitation may well come from envy or covetousness.

In any case, there are three traps in imitation:

1. Imitation cancels out the individual worth of what is imitated because it can be duplicated.
2. Imitation cancels out the uniqueness of the imitation, because of the prior uniqueness of what is imitated.
3. Imitation questions the individuality of the imitator by denying his or her right to see or say something in a different way. Hence, the imitator is nothing more than an imitation of all other imitators.

In sum, this first principle suggests to us that musical and artistic action should be driven by what happened at the dawn of creation when everything was new and surprising, integral and whole, and, in the very best sense of the word, abstract. This is another way of saying that artists and musicians, in one way or another, have a fundamental obligation to participate in creative "firstness." However, this need not mean that music and art should only be "abstract" or nonreferential. A second principle is therefore necessary.

2. *The creation was not only originally imagined but continued. That is, there was not just a first strawberry but countless others, no two of which are alike.* The second strawberry did not imitate but *re-presented the first.* Re-presenting is a way of depicting the same thing differently, of "saying it in other words." Re-presenting, in the most creative sense of the word, is just as difficult as originating. This concept is quite different from the platonic concept of ideal and real. In the biblical frame of reference, there is not an "ideal" strawberry of which all the rest are imitations or shadows. Rather, every strawberry is essential, individual and real, even as the very first one was. Ideal form is not "out there" and imitative content "right here." On the contrary, real form is another way of describing real content.

We must remember that a true artist does not attempt to portray something the way it is but the way he or she sees it to be. The quality of a landscape painting does not depend on how well the landscape is replicated but on the individual vision the artist brings to the re-presentation. The original landscape is simply a model— one way of depiction. The next creative step is up to the artist and his or her capability to imagine a difference. The artist, as a created creator, can say, "Dear Creator, now that you have shown me your way, I shall try to show you mine."

The third principle follows out of the reality of our created individuality.

3. *Since artistic style may be defined as the language of individual consistency, there can be as many different re-presentations of a*

*given object as there are creative individuals. Consequently,
uniqueness of personal style is far more crucial than the artistic or
musical procedures and systems we choose.* Examples may be drawn
from any art form, but one from music will suffice. At the end of
the nineteenth century, particularly in the music of Richard
Wagner, it was said that the concept of tonality was exhausted. But
in the early twentieth century, through the thought and musical
work of Arnold Schönberg, a radical concept developed. Pitches
could be organized, not around a tonal center, but in orderly
relation to each other, each pitch being equal to all others. The
force of this concept was such that every serious composer since
then has had to reckon with it one way or another.

Despite this, a significant number of composers then and now
have continued to use the "older" tonal process while showing
striking originality. Why? Because the sheer force of individual creativity can dominate the system chosen. Individual style is not
system-dependent. To say otherwise negates the importance of this
fact of creation: As long as there are no two creative people alike—
and God's way of creating assures us of that—no artistic or musical
system can be exhausted. If an artist or musician chooses to change
systems, it may simply be that his or her own thinking has changed
or possibly become exhausted. In the meantime, others continue to
originate within the system. In the final analysis, there are two
creative ways we can approach artistic systems and concepts. We
will either be conservative (imagining and crafting within a known
system) or radical (imagining a new system and crafting within it).
In either case, the issue of individual creativity remains constant.

But these three principles about artistic activity include an
interesting wrinkle. Maybe the first two principles are superficially
different ways of saying the same thing. Artists are finite, even the
best of them. They are bound by the creation. They cannot step
outside of it, and there is no way that they can ever out-imagine the
Creator. They are a created part of all the conceivable textures,
colors, shapes, densities, nuances, and qualities that the uncreated
Creator first imagined and crafted. Therefore anything ever painted,

danced, composed, sculpted, or chiseled may be only a personal stylization, extension, or translation of something already in existence, whether the artist has actually seen it or not. Being created in the image of God gives artists a unique capacity for seeing *into* all of the creation without physically having to see *all* of it. Creative vision is more than optical vision, physical hearing, or technique. It rests in the unexplainable mystery of human beings created in the image of their Creator (*imago dei*).

Time after time we discover these links between God's handiwork and our own. A work of art, initially thought to be abstract or nonrepresentational, turns out to be "like" the cross-section of a cell under intense magnification or the tracings of protonic motion photographed in an accelerator or the elegantly "choreographed" courting rites of a tropical bird. Once we get away from the surface beauty of the creation—what we look at day after day: the pine trees, the dandelions, and clouds; once we begin to see *into* it, way down, out beyond, and yet further into—we begin to understand how even the most "radical" art, music, or dance is a human paraphrase of something that the Creator did first. At the same time, we must remember that this paraphrasing is not a sneaky way of saying that God created our art and music and then breathed it into being through us. ("God gave me this song.") Nor is it another way of saying that all of this composed art and music was somehow "out there" waiting to be created by mortals. This creative work of ours is real and it can be downright beautiful. It is only when we compare it to the work of the one whose creative speech is transcendentally articulate that ours pales in comparison. Just read Job, chapters 38 to 41.

Musicians do not learn from the creation in quite the same way visual artists do. There are no fugues or twelve-bar blues "out there" for us to use as models or to re-present. Even so, the principle suggested in the difference between the first day and all other days pertains to musical practice as well. In music, there are two poles: the strange and the familiar, somewhat analogous to the difference between the abstract and the representational in art. Radically different music may be just as difficult to accept as abstract art, when its harmonic practices, textures, structures, and colors are completely separated from what we have grown used to. This kind of music is best received in the spirit of the first day of creation. We must learn to live in the wonder—even shock—of that day, no matter how disturbed, stretched, or even threatened we might be. Creative musicians have every right to thrive within the spirit of that day and to produce musical works that honor God by following hard after his originating ways.

But this is not all. Many musical days have followed the first day. These are the days of innovative conservatism, nuanced repetition, paraphrase, and variation. While the first day of creation is absolutely essential to the practice of music, so are all the other days. And the most balanced artistic communities—and these must surely include the Christian ones—are those that seek both the avant-garde and the conservative; the new, the disturbing, and the most inventively familiar.

God's Creation, Stylistic Pluralism, and Music Making

The creation, at first glance, appears to be full of anomalies. Because there are lobsters and hummingbirds, deserts and rain forests, turtles and people, we might be tempted to believe that a mixture of creative opinions has been at work, an assortment of deities, if you will, who have either compromised with each other or concluded their business in outright disagreement. How could the same Someone think up a hippopotamus and then turn around and imagine an orchid? Is God inconsistent? Does God have any taste? Or is he a Creator whose sense of rightness and beauty are so complete that we will have a more comprehensive way of integrating all of the supposed anomalies and contradictions in human creativity? Is there a way for us to see if or how the music of Eric Clapton or Beethoven can find a place among the musics of Japanese *kabuki*, the Balinese gamelan, the songs of Stephen Foster, an anonymous dreamer of songs in Africa, J. S. Bach, and

Blind Lemon Jefferson? We need to find ways to validate artistic pluralism without becoming so sloppy as to allow anything.

There is but one God, one author of all creation. The astonishing variety in the creation, the juxtapositions of delicacy and roughness, fragility and resilience, grotesqueness and grace, plainness and ornamentation, issued out of a singularly consistent mind, given over to making things well and, in their peculiar way, beautiful.

When we speak of the beauty of the creation we must remember that we usually make selective choices among all of the things that God called good—things that to God as well as their own kind are eminently desirable. We often choose parts of the creation the way we choose art and music: some we like, some we don't. This is all right as long as we don't imply that God's creation can be graded according to our limited concepts of beauty and worth. In doing this, we can overlook the fundamental wonder and beauty of all creation along with the sum of the essential wholeness and integrity of each created thing. Thus we may have no more aesthetic right to say that a sunset is more beautiful than an artichoke than we do to say that classical music is more beautiful than jazz or Gothic preferable to Bauhaus. Perhaps we need to compare Gothic with Gothic, jazz with jazz, folk with folk, and so on, before we get involved in trying to decide among them.

We can conclude that God has but one personal style, expended in endless variety. From this we learn that singularity of process and consistency of style can issue in endless variety. If God can create all this variety with one personal style, so can we. Bach did not assume one creative personality for his secular music and another for his church music. He might have employed different techniques, processes, and even vocabularies, but he remained Johann Sebastian Bach throughout. He had his own unique musical thumbprint. That is why Bach cannot sound like Handel and Ella Fitzgerald cannot sound like Sarah Vaughan. These artists must remain themselves, through and through. Their way of joining and coloring sounds remains personal and unique. This is not just because of precocity or genius. Each was created individually different in the image of the one whose creation bears a personal stamp throughout the whole handiwork.

There is thus a profound difference between creative individuality and multiple creative styles. Honest musicians, whatever their level of ability and training, wherever they are in their creative sojourn, are free to understand that individuality can issue in any number of styles and dialects. They should be free to pursue stylistic variety, especially if they plan to serve in a variety of musical environments. They must understand that there is nothing wrong with these shifts and changes, as long as they cherish and maintain personal integrity.

God's way of creating demonstrates that multiple styles and dialects are not an indication of some kind of creative ambiguity or a compromise of personal integrity. All musicians and artists may freely turn to their creator and to the creation, observing God at work—creating riotously, popularly, seriously, multi-idiomatically, lumberingly, elegantly, humorously, profoundly, prickly, and smoothly. Then they must go back to their keyboards, easels, potter's wheels, and choreographic charts and do the same. If they do—honestly and personally—if they put integrity of mind and heart to work, if they allow their imagination, wisdom, and personal ways to consort with each other, the world will be all the richer, all the more pleasured, and all the more disturbed. If the same God can think up a cucumber and a falcon, the same potter can make a vase and a free-form object, the same poet can make a simple couplet or an extended drama, and the same composer a Scripture song or a symphony.

God's Creation: Function, Worth, and Music Making

The creation is the best example for the complete integration of worth and function. Everything that God creates has intrinsic worth, and everything that has worth functions. God calls this total integration good: beauty, worth, usefulness, and function are united at every turn; they do not slip into and out of coordination with each other. A sunset is beautiful in its own right, but it is also a consortium of usefulness: the gilded clouds hold moisture; light is refracted and colored by the atmosphere we breathe. The sun warms the earth, controls its weather, gives light, and in its daily absence allows cool and dark. A rose, magnificent in its own right, aesthetically outdistancing anything that a Gauguin could paint, has medicinal value. It cooperates with other flowering plants by sharing its pollen, while honeybees, going from one to another, make a substance that is useful to them, to animals, and to humans. When the rose dies, its function continues as its petals drop, nourishing and fertilizing the earth in order that succeeding roses and other growing things can flourish.

Any serious discussion of music making is bound to include the subject of function or functionalism. In Western classicism, a concept has gradually evolved that art should have no other function than to be perceived on its own terms and for its own sake. Consequently, institutionalized settings for art—concerts, exhibits, museums, and theaters—are virtually considered separate places, supposedly free of the kind of functionalism found in the outside world. At the same time, functionalists maintain that music and the rest of the arts do not have to be so isolated and singularly perceived. According to them, the arts should be useful, near at hand, and at work with other activities. Advertisers, for instance, use music and art to assist in the marketing and selling of products, and the church expects its art forms to serve the liturgy, even to assist in the inducement of worship.

Both positions, art for art's sake and functionalism, when taken to extremes, are problematic. The concept of art for its own sake often leads to snobbery, arrogance, and convoluted intellectualism. It also overlooks the facts of history, namely that much of the art that now stands alone was once meant to function along with, or even be backgrounded by, other activities. However, art as function can easily end up in mediocrity and a cheapened sense of utilitarianism. And many functionalists hide good art so completely in the functional that the viewers/listeners have no idea of the real significance of the art.

Proponents of art for art's sake overlook the following ways in which art functions, even in its best moments.

1. *As it is being perceived, art functions as an object of intellectual analysis, criticism, and contextualization.* In Western culture, these activities have come to have their own separate importance and worth, to the extent they often turn out to substitute for a meaningful encounter with art itself. This then raises the question of what functions for what.

2. *Even in the most "cultured" musical events, music will cofunction with other activities.* For example, a formal concert may function as a reason for wearing artistically noticeable clothing and jewelry, meeting friends, or showing cultural intelligence. The concert hall itself may be an architectural and acoustical masterpiece with every right to be perceived in its own way and for its own worth. And it must function so that people may be properly and comfortably seated and the music clearly heard.

3. *Performance itself may function primarily as a means for comparing performances with each other, instead of perceiving the music irrespective of the performance.* We listen less to Beethoven's Fifth Symphony or Shakespeare's *Hamlet* than to Leonard Bernstein's or Laurence Olivier's *rendition* of it. The emphasis has been subtly shifted from content to production. Consequently, musical content ends up being a function of performance instead of the opposite.

4. *In all contexts of worship, art and music can have no higher role than to function—to be at work—within the liturgy.* As in the creation itself, neither quality nor function have independent status. Art is not for its own sake, nor can function be validated apart from a concern for quality.

The functionalist's errors can be twofold.

1. *The functionalist often seems to have little problem overlooking artistic quality and worth in order to obtain results.* The irony here is that the result to be sought may itself be noble and of the highest quality. For example, nothing could be more important than the salvation of a soul, and nothing should call for higher quality of life

than the Christian life. Thus the efforts expended to achieve the result should not contradict this. By contrast, if the result to be sought is cheap or flawed and high-quality art is used to obtain the result, quality is still being overlooked.

2. *The functionalist often denies the prophetic, originating quality of art.* Artistic and musical perception then become matters of repetition, conditioned reflex, familiarity, and even mind control. The extreme of this approach is found in totalitarian regimes in which artistic content has no interior rights and must completely subordinate itself to the ideological propositions to which the state has dedicated itself. In this case, artists are reduced to being mouthpieces, and if they attempt to step outside of this role they are severely punished. This same thing, without the overt punishment, can happen in church music when the *sole* purpose of music and art is to perpetuate familiarity, be a tool of the gospel, or preserve the "right" conditions for worship, with no room for artistic vision or change. As a result, many honest church musicians are either pressured to compromise or forced out of the practice itself.

The issue of function and worth can be taken further. Even though God meant the creation to be used and consumed, every speck of it has been carefully and lovingly made. Roses die quickly and apples are eaten in a trice. Yet they take months of time and huge expenditures of energy to grow fully. Richly grained wood, which might have taken decades to come to maturity, simply furnishes fuel for the fireside. They are created the same way; there is no division of purpose; there are no two qualities of workmanship, the one for the immediate, the other for the ages.

We live in a throwaway culture. When something is intended to be used up quickly and discarded, it is not as carefully made as that which is meant to last. Just as there is throwaway technology, there is throwaway art—art for the moment. Lasting power is irrelevant and the presence of quality is often in inverse proportion to length of use. At the same time, those who make music and art "for the ages" are, in their own way, as guilty as those who make art for immediate disposal. Both overlook the importance of their contemporaries and surroundings. Throwaway artists litter culture and force on people things that demean and dull their sensitivity, while those who look only to future vindication overlook the importance of serving and enriching the very people around them. The "immediatists" worship usefulness and the "futurists," vindication.

The lesson for music makers, especially Christians, is obvious. We should not merely "grind it out" because we know that "it's just for prayer meeting" or subvert quality and integrity in the interest of "communication." We must always remember that the very subversion of quality communicates something about the kind of gospel we are trying to propagate. If we faithfully followed God's example, there would no longer be the crassness and cynicism of the throwaway or the false pomp and pretense of art for the ages. Nor would the Holy Spirit be continually pestered to turn poor work into blessed work. The Christian musician has no right whatsoever to assume that anything other than the mind of Christ and the Creatorhood of God should guide very note composed, arranged, played, and sung. This is nothing other than good stewardship. The reason is simple: God the Creator has made it clear that function and worth, usefulness and integrity, are to be joined in every action.

God's Creation, Simplicity, Complexity, and Music Making

A galaxy and a blade of grass may differ, but only in the expanse of quality. This should give us no excuse for overlooking the wonder in a blade of grass. The galaxy and the grass are put together in the same way: elemental particles are chained together, in the one case to make something small and, in the other, to make something exceedingly vast. It is the elemental parts, the "simple particles," that, yet to be explained, remain the greater mystery.

We can make the same mistake with simplicity and complexity that we do with worth and function when we see one as better than the other. What is simplicity in human creativity? Complexity? If complexity means more and simplicity less, then the final movement of Beethoven's Ninth Symphony is complex and Brahms's "Lullaby" is simple. If complex means complicated and simplicity clear, then Karl Barth's writing is complex and C. S. Lewis simple. And if the cathedral of Notre Dame is complex, the great pyramids of Egypt are simple. Which of these is better? More profound? Is Paul McCartney's "Yesterday" or one of Matisse's simple line drawings of less quality than Schubert's Quintet in C Major or Da Vinci's *Mona Lisa?* Which is more profound, the brevity of the Golden Rule or the cumulative rhetoric of the book of Romans?

Great art and great music do not come about just by amassing detail. Instead, true artistry is more a matter of exquisite timing and spacing among all of the parts: how to make something, how much of it to make, and when to change or stop. Take, for instance, the hymn tune "Austria" (sung to "Glorious Things of Thee Are Spoken") or "Georgia on My Mind" or "Amazing Grace." These are relatively short and simple pieces of music. Each uses less than the allotted twelve pitches of our musical system; they are easy to sing, they are eloquent, and they have been crafted in ways that can elude the best of us. They just don't wear out. Yet, anybody who knows anything about the relation of musical analysis to aesthetic analysis understands that only a few "turns" within each one can spell the difference between mere goodness and greatness.

For instance, in "Austria" we can tamper with its greatness by changing just two notes: making the high F in the fourth-from-last measure into a C, and the C in the eleventh measure into an A.[5] Everything remains the same. The result is still quite musical, but not eminently so. Just two notes make the difference. Likewise, if an artist were to make a few minuscule changes around Mona Lisa's mouth, she would be robbed of the mysterious smile. Yet the Mona Lisa is complex and "Austria" is simple. Each is great; each possesses a peculiar uniqueness. The one is distinguished from the other only by the expanse of quality.

Simple musical creativity is no less important to the whole of human creativity than the simplicities of creation are to its whole.

But this does not mean that we rest content with musical simplicity any more than we exclude the galaxy because the blade of grass is easier to take in. As elegant and enigmatic as the simple may be, its pleasure is comparatively brief. By contrast, the complex demands extended discipline, attention, and memory. In turn it offers a different and deeper satisfaction, extended over the entire expanse of the particular creative act. The complete person needs both. Just as the blade of grass points to the deeper wonder of the galaxy, so must the simple tune point to the mystery of the oratorio.

The Incarnation, Human Creativity, and Music Making

When Jesus Christ became flesh, he became a part of the creation in exactly the same way that every human being has. That is, even though he was fully God, he became fully human. Consequently, he had to depend on the creation, subject himself to its laws, and make his way through its beauties, anomalies, and disruptions just like the very ones whom he came to redeem. Had he become a musician instead of a carpenter, he would have had no particular jump on music making by being the Son of God. The overtone series would not have acted differently for him; he would have had to receive training—fumbling here and recouping there, just as he doubtless did when he first learned to walk or take his first turns at the carpenter's bench. These growing pains were just as real for the Son of God as for us. The only difference was that Jesus did his learning, growing, and maturing sinlessly and perfectly, but this does not mean that he was an instant learner. Nor does it mean that, had he made music, it would have been earthshakingly ahead of its time or culture.

This brings us to a principle—an unexplainable mystery—about which the Scriptures speak plainly and directly. This principle is the final guide for all human creativity, whatever task it undertakes. In Philippians (2:3–11) Christ is described as having emptied himself. This not the place, nor am I theologically equipped, to delve into the full theological and doctrinal complexities of the Incarnation.

Suffice it to say, when Christ came to earth, he somehow was able to limit—to empty—himself as God, while remaining fully God, yet being fully human.

In a way, God was simplified. And as with so many simplicities, this deepens the mystery. While this emptying means everything to our redemption, it applies to our artistic and musical creativity with nearly equal force. An analogy may help. Let's say that before Christ became human, he could be likened to a symphony, in all of its complexity and power—magnificence carried out over a grand expanse. But when he became human, he became a folk tune, simple and shortened. In this, he lost nothing of his Godhood, his eternal character, his attributes, absolute purity, and changeless excellence. His becoming a folk tune was not a compromise, a dilution, a put-down, or a thinning out. Nor did it mean that he canceled out his prior being as a symphony. Instead, He willingly gave up this prerogative, humbly convinced that he should not grasp at it. Becoming a folk tune was a uniqueness in itself, with its own wholeness, integrity, and usefulness. Putting it this way prevents us from saying that a folk tune is a thinned-out or reduced symphony. Rather, it is an *emptied* symphony, completely possessed of its own wholeness, integrity, and uniqueness.

Thus for the musician and the artist there is a difference between putting creative prerogatives aside and compromising or diluting them. Christ showed us this difference, and the true artist and musician—may we now say, the servant musician and artist—must learn this principle completely. Each musician must come to experience the dignity, rightness, and eventual joy of putting things aside, of emptying oneself and taking the form of a servant. Such musicians must be able to move back and forth, gracefully, servingly, and willingly, from the symphony to the folk tune; back and forth without complaint, compromise, or snobbery, without the conceit that doing an oratorio is somehow more worthy or more deserving than doing a hymn tune. All servant musicians must be able to be in creative transit, serving this community and challenging that one, all the while showing grace, power, elegance, and imagination.

To empty ourselves the way Christ did is to remain the same all the while. This means that integrity, conscience, imagination, worth, and excellence are to be as evident in the tune as in the symphony. The lessons of simplicity and complexity, worth and usefulness, variety and unity, familiarity and strangeness, function and quality are all driven by the larger lesson of the emptying in the Incarnation. The servant musician, living this way, is finally learning the lesson of artistic wisdom. He or she is learning to acquire the gift of functional integrity, which is nothing other than the ability to maintain excellence, high purpose, and artfulness in the fulfillment of any creative task in any context to which God voices a call.

Which is the greater mystery, that Christ is God or that he could empty himself while remaining God? Likewise, which is the greater mystery, that we are artistically creative or that we can remain just as fully creative while emptying ourselves?

The Creation, Human Creativity, Community, and Music Making

God creates out of nothing (*ex nihilo*), which God is not, into something, which God also is not. We create out of something (*ex quō*) in which we somehow participate, into other things, in which we continue to participate. And though we are not incarnate in what we make, we are still a part of the creation—of the dust. We must use the creation and in responsible ways change, improve, and add to it.

We are thus not only utterly dependent on God—on God's being and actions—but on the creation itself, in all of its reality, potential, richness, diversity, content, and process. We depend on other people—those presently around us and those who have lived before us. Linked in countless ways, we imagine and make. Shut off from these communities, we become quite helpless. The reason is simple: we cannot create out of nothing. Our abilities to imagine and craft, as remarkable as they are, are dependent and limited. We need raw materials, precedent, models, examples, and advice. We must experiment, learn, sketch, reject, develop, synthesize, start over, refine, and revise. And we need enormous amounts of time and very large wastebaskets. As much as we like to think of ourselves as being original—and some people are startlingly so—we must own up to the impossibility of being creatively productive without recognizing our dependence on community. And the more creative and hardworking we are, the more we will draw on what lies around us. Musical and artistic provincialism are the result of a failure to reach out into, celebrate, and use the rich imagination of those who have been individually gifted to do what we cannot.

Let's look at it this way. Had Beethoven lived in the Renaissance, he could not have composed the music he did. He would no doubt have been a composer, but his music would have sounded vastly different. His music did not come about irrespective of context but in the midst of it. In order for him to do what he did and to bring his creative individuality to its highest, he first needed Mozart; Mozart needed Haydn; and then because Haydn outlived Mozart, Haydn eventually turned out to be influenced by Mozart. This same Haydn turned out to be Beethoven's counterpoint teacher; but Haydn also needed Stamitz and his contemporaries; they needed the sons of Bach; they in turn needed their father; their father needed Buxtehude, and Buxtehude needed his musical forebears. And so on, down through history, back into prototypical music making. Even this is too simplistic because the community of composers must be woven into other communities: ecclesiastical, economic, sociological, political, familial, geographic, procedural, and technological. Each of these affected and was affected by every other in nearly untraceable ways. The whole inevitably affected how and what the individual thought up and crafted. If we substitute rock music for Beethoven, we come up with parallel complexities and contextual matrices. As different as this music is and as important as it has become, it was not made in a vacuum.

Wherever we go in the annals of musical activity, we will discover this one thing: people make things out of, into, for (or against) community. Musical creativity is contextual. The wider the context, the more rich the options and the more varied the results. Even a tribal musician, geographically separated away from the next nearest tribe, let alone from the wider world, will make choices from within the world he or she knows. But it is still a world, made out of the contextual stuff that precedes and surrounds it. And each creative act adds just that much more to the world within which it comes about.

This concept of community reaches its highest in the body of Christ, within which all of the parts are in eminent need of each other. Whatever the foot does, the head feels; whatever is taken away from one part will result in a deprivation in all the parts. When a Christian musician goes about making music, the concept of the community/body should drive every note and every moment in which every note is heard. And the only object for every Christian musician is to build the body up into the stature and fullness of its head, Jesus Christ.

If musicians assume themselves to be above the community, they end up denying the very reality that has made their way of creating possible. An analogy from the physical creation will illustrate this. There are two kinds of force, centripetal and centrifugal. Centripetal force urges things inward, toward a powerful center. Centrifugal force urges things outward. Musicians can act centripetally, expecting everything and everybody to come their way. They can be centrifugal, continually giving themselves without taking much in.

Or they can be both. They can drink in from as many sources as possible, giving thanks for the rich world of musical creativity, drawing people in and serving them. Then, linked to the body of Christ and obligated to a world community, they fling themselves outward as servants, shepherds, helpers, teachers, bards, and prophets. This grand combination of drinking in and giving out is the best way Christian musicianship can be defined, whether it takes place in church, the concert hall, the home, the jazz club, coffeehouse, public school, or mission field. The creation exemplifies it, the gospel commands it, people need it, and Christ lived it perfectly.

NOTES

1. This definition helps clarify the meaning of crafting. Crafting is the actual making of something after it has been thought up. It may be undertaken by the imaginer or by a craftsperson who must work according to the plans of the imaginer. Yet craftspersons are not limited just to crafting, for they may have to think up and make tools and systems for finishing the task that was originally given them, and in other areas of their lives they regularly engage in thinking up and doing. Thus being a craftsperson by trade by no means shuts down the reality of being creative by instinct.

2. In this section as well as in other places throughout the book, the reader will notice a number of references to God using the pronouns *he* or *him*. While I have tried to avoid using gender specific language wherever possible, I have felt it necessary to employ these pronouns for two reasons. First, in the scripture passage upon which this particular section is based (Exodus 3:1–14), as well as in others similar to it, God is referred to unequivocally as *he*. Second, I generally take the use of *he* or *him* to refer to God's fatherhood, not his manhood, and certainly not his sexual being. To me, motherhood and fatherhood, in the most profound and comprehensive sense, transcend the more gender specific connotations of womanhood and manhood. In fact, true manhood and true womanhood should never be limited to maleness or femaleness, even among human beings. I firmly believe that the best women and the best men, as well as the best mothers and fathers, of this world are not just males or females, but completely human, participating in, and showing forth, the best of each other's personal qualities.

3. Carrying this thought further, God creates oak trees and oak trees are oak trees. But God has created us in the divine image. Further, God has begotten an only Son, who, as a man, was made in God's image while being Very God of Very God. Those who have been created in the image of God and then have returned to God through the only begotten Son are then called children of God. They are thus created both in the image of God *and* begotten of God. The redeemed are not just created beings. They have become partakers of the things of God: joint heirs with Christ, finite children of an infinite Creator.

4. In this section, the implications for the visual arts are so enormous that we will be alluding to them more than usual. I thought seriously of adding an independent section on the visual arts but decided that the present approach would be more useful, if only to highlight the integrative nature of all the arts, especially as to how principles that appear to apply more particularly to one art form can assist in explaining another. Another reason for emphasizing the visual arts is because the extraordinary richness of the creation has influenced the content of the visual arts far more than its sonic richness has affected music. When we say that God is the supreme artist and God's creation is the supreme artwork, we almost inevitably have the visible creation in mind. On the other hand, when we think about music, we do not usually refer to God as the supreme musician. Instead, we say something such as God created music, but instead of referring to the music in the creation to demonstrate this, we refer to our own. Does this mean that there is more visual than sonic completeness in the creation, or does it mean that we have somehow bypassed a deeper fundamental presence of music in the creation itself? I do not know a good answer,

and in a way it is not all that important for the present discussion. What is important is the larger principle that has already been stated, namely that God both imagines and crafts out of nothing.

5. Key of F major.

Chapter 2

WHAT DOES MUSIC MEAN?

The confusion concerning music as a means of communication clearly arises from a lack of understanding of what music really signifies . . . Not only do we find . . . music essentially indefinable, but the more precisely we try to define it, the more unsatisfactory the result.

—ROGER SESSIONS

Happy is he who does not condemn himself in what he approves.
—ROMANS 14:22b (NASB)

This is a true story. Not many years ago, a young man became heavily involved in a satanic cult. This was no offhanded cult, but one of profoundly serious intention. The liturgies used were complex and sophisticated and the devotees were adamant in their dedication. In short, the cult completely dictated the lifestyles and worldviews of its adherents. In addition to the words, gestures, and vestments of the liturgy, this cult regularly used a certain kind of music. The musicians were dedicated to good music making and set about to prove this at every musical turn in the liturgy.

This young man was somehow reached by the gospel and gloriously converted to Christianity. His worship was transformed and turned right side up; his devotion to Jesus Christ was eager and faithful. He left the cult and began to seek out a church in which everything said and done would nurture him and wrest him from any and all of the clutches in which his former practices still tried to hold him.

He sought the counsel of his new Christian friends and decided upon a well-known church in the community—one known both for its attention to the things of God as well as to the practice of the best music and art. All was well, until on a particular Sunday the organist played a special composition, one well known and loved by the rest of the congregation. The young man was traumatized. Everything that smacked of the old inverted satanic system flooded back in on him. He could do nothing but rush from the church, nearly overcome with fear and dread. The music was by Johann Sebastian Bach, a composer whose music, to many people, represents some of the noblest music for Christian worship. To this young man, however, it was not noble at all, but rather epitomized all that was evil, horrible, and anti-Christian, for it was Bach that the cult leaders had chosen to be the musical mainstay of their liturgy. To the young man, this great music was a barrier of such magnitude that worship was not possible.

Human beings have assigned moral value to art and music from time immemorial, and it has affected artistic and musical practice in countless ways. Consider the following.

When pipe organs were introduced into the church, Christians were up in arms. How could this monstrosity, taken from pagan contexts, be anything other than an instrument of the devil?

The Roman Catholic church for centuries, by official decree, divided music into sacred and secular categories, allowing the former and forbidding the latter in the liturgy. These decrees were applied to masses, motets, and other liturgical compositions by well-known and well-intentioned composers. The only problem with forbidden pieces was that they were perceived to be secular rather than sacred in nature.

Salvador Dali's painting *Christ on the Cross* or his *Last Supper* are considered to be straightforwardly pagan and secularly humanistic by some people, while to others they breathe something fresh and daring, even Christian, into older prototypes.

Many Christians condemn rock music, not just for being openly non-Christian, but because they consider it responsible for causing immoral behavior. Others not only condone it but adopt it wholesale as being the most appropriate music for Christian worship.

New Age music is said by some to be the embodiment of Eastern cults, to be avoided like the plague by all Christians, while some Christian musicians freely experiment with its idioms as a part of their worship and witness.

Returning missionaries describe the music of tribal musicians as satanic, capable of leading its participants into all sorts of strange and suspect behavior. And for that matter, new Christians in these same societies cannot bring themselves to use the music of their former ways, a curiously parallel situation to the young man who could no longer listen to the music of Bach. In these instances there is nearly wholesale fear of rhythms, harmonies, instruments, and gestures.

The church has for centuries waged one brush war after another over the question of whether or how art and music "mean"—what it means to borrow styles, forms, processes, tunes, techniques, textures, shapes, gestures, and instruments from secular sources. Presently the debate centers around rock and New Age music. A few decades ago it was about jazz and popular ballads.

And so it goes and has gone, back through the decades and centuries, across cultures, and clean through denominational, sectarian, and doctrinal practices. Despite the numberless instances and their seeming diversity, one common thread runs throughout. At the time of the borrowing, the war rages, often quite bitterly and divisively. Then as time passes, the war dies down. The previously condemned becomes merely questionable, if not outrightly sacred. After all, what about pipe organs? (Or today is it synthesizers?) Now considered to be a churchly instrument, who would dare secularize it?

What does art mean anyhow? Do art and music carry truth messages? Is a painting ethical or a fugue moral? Is using music composed by a non-Christian any different than using a building designed by an architect who happens to be an atheist or purchasing an Easter outfit designed by a nihilist? Are twentieth-century—or in just a few years, twenty-first-century—art and music more suspect than their predecessors? Does our culture's greater distance from Christ mean that its artworks are proportionately more suspect? If so, what is left for today's Christian artists to do? If not, why is the church so reluctant to enjoy the rich variety of style, vocabulary, process, shape, and medium that issues from every quarter of the globe?

There is a further question: Does music carry meaning the same way as a painting? Do all art forms carry meaning the same way, and can they carry propositionally clear messages with equal clarity and precision? If we decide that all art carries moral messages and that all art is equally "sermonic"—capable of standing in place of the gospel, evangelizing, prophesying, and reforming society and church—then we must conclude that particular artistic types and vocabularies are right only for a particular religion or ethical system. If we decide that art does not carry moral messages, then Christian thinkers must take greater care in developing a view of the arts that articulates clear-cut distinctions among the arts and that explains why the young man spoken of at the beginning of the chapter suffered the contextual trauma that he did while others, sitting in the same church, listening to the same music, did not.

From here on out, I take the position that, with certain excep-tions,[1] art and especially music are morally relative and inherently incapable of articulating, for want of a better term, truth speech. They are essentially neutral in their ability to express belief, creed, moral and ethical exactitudes, or even worldview. I also assume that, no matter how passionately artists may believe what they believe or try to show these beliefs in what they imagine and craft, their art remains purposefully "dumb." Further, I maintain that artists and their works can be separated and their works are to be understood simply as handiwork. Even so, artists remain personally accountable for what they believe, how they behave, and for the reasons they make their art and music the way they do. Finally, I will assume that Christians are biblically justified in fully celebrating artistic activity of the most diverse sort, including that which may have been created in downright unbelief.

Why Truth Is Not Beauty and Beauty Is Not Truth

In chapter 1 we made the point that the creator is not the creation and the music maker is not the music. Now we must consider this principle from another direction: God's handiwork is not the same as God's truth. To equate them in any way is to commit the same error equating God's person with the creation. The coupling of truth and beauty is as old as platonic thought and as young as countless repetitions of it in aesthetic treatises, college catalogues, and variously romanticized orations. But truth is not beauty and beauty is not truth.

Beauty is a quality, an idealized abstraction. Truth is not an abstraction or simply a quality. It is real, revealed, self-inhering, immediately useful, imminent, propositionally articulated, and absolute. There is no such thing as an ideal truth and a real truth, a heavenly truth and an earthly truth. Nor is truth a quality applied to something else to make it truthful. It is a completeness to which all else is in some way subject.

There may be degrees of beauty but not of truth. An artwork may be more beautiful or less beautiful than another, even though each may be considered to be in good taste and quite desirable. There may be legitimate debate over whether Bach's music is more beautiful than Mozart's, let alone whether a Rembrandt painting is more beautiful than a Shakespeare sonnet. But in the case of truth, there is no such debate. There is a final and absolute reference point, there is a person who is truth, by whose word all things have been called into being, who is revealed in the Scriptures and finally and fully in the person of Jesus Christ, the incarnate Word, the yes and amen to every word of God. Christians are then called to be living epistles, living out the speech of God, while simultaneously being indwelt by the very Word of God. These are the eternal realities of truth. They transcend time, culture, and human invention.

The beauty of God is not aesthetic beauty but moral and ethical beauty. The beauty of the creation is not moral beauty; it is aesthetic beauty, artifactual beauty. Aesthetic beauty lies in the *way* and the quality with which something is made or said. Truth lies in *what* is said. Thus a statement may be aesthetically suspect and still be true or be untrue and still be aesthetically beautiful.

If beauty and truth were equal, then ugliness and untruth would likewise be equal. An artistically inferior gospel song, correctly stating truth about salvation, would have to be rejected out of hand because of its aesthetic error. Yet we know that it is possible to come to a full knowledge of the truth even though what we hear may be embedded in mediocrity. Truth can override aesthetic lapses, but aesthetic lapses cannot cancel out truth. Untruth, no matter how beautifully stated, remains untruth. Beauty cannot redeem it.

If truth can override beauty, why spend so much time making something beautiful? Some have answered this question with bad art, which to them is justified because it gets the job done. "Just look at the results," they say. "If God is blessing it, who are you to criticize it and why should I change it?" Others take the correct view: "Because God does all things well, we should likewise do well. While we strive to be truthful, we will strive to state truth beautifully. And in proceeding this way, I honor God by trying to work as God does. In the meantime, God is free to work any time, in any place, and in any way at all."

Our task is to strive for quality with all our might, not to maneuver God into acting more effectively, but simply because we are commanded to. Therefore, if we *knowingly* continue in mediocrity just because we seem to be effective, we will be as severely judged as those who assume that excellence *per se* will cause God to act all the more quickly and powerfully.

Revelation and Creation, the Alternative to Truth and Beauty

We need a new paradigm that separates truth and beauty yet allows each its proper place. I call this *revelation and creation. According to this paradigm, the maker and what is made are not interchangeable or equatable, and beauty can apply to everything made and said.* Thus truth can be beautifully stated and lived out; things can be beautifully made. Something less than truthfully done is sin, whereas something less than beautifully made—even though it might be extremely unpleasant—can be dealt with simply as a lapse in aesthetic judgment.

Among the many passages of Scripture referring to the Creator and his handiwork, two stand out: Romans 1:19–20 and Psalm 19. The Romans passage is the more direct of the two: "For since the creation of the world God's invisible qualities—His eternal power and divine nature—have been clearly seen, being understood from what has been made" (NIV).

Psalm 19 begins similarly: "The heavens are telling the glory of God; And their expanse is declaring the work of His hands. Day to day pours forth speech, And night to night reveals knowledge" (NASB).

At first glance, these passages might appear to say that God's handiwork *does* speak like God does, that in the creation there *is* speech, there *is* knowledge. However, when examined more closely, these passages do not make that kind of case. Both passages make it clear that God's handiwork is limited in what it can say.

The Romans passage argues for the existence and supremacy of a Creator, his power, and his deity. But it does *not* say that when we view the creation in unsuppressed conscience we can tell what God is thinking, what God's truth comprises, or how God saves. The passage only suggests that those who see the creation for what it is must face up to the knowledge of a supreme Creator and are responsible to turn to God, to listen to what *God* says, and to do so with repentance and worship. It speaks of God's handiwork as a message *of the existence of* a glorious Creator rather than a message *describing* the Creator attribute by attribute. The implication is that once we turn from the handiwork to the Creator, we will hear him speaking directly, revelationally, and truthfully—*in ways of which the handiwork is completely incapable.* If God's handiwork were capable of speaking the way God does, there would be no need for the Scriptures or the Incarnation. Then we would be left with pantheism (The creation is God) or panlogoism (The creation is God's Word).

Psalm 19 adds a further dimension. It states that the heavens declare the creator's glory and that the days and nights pour forth speech and knowledge—a sure parallel to the Romans passage. But then an element of ambiguity appears. The Hebrew becomes unclear. The days and nights pour forth speech, and some translations say that there is no place where their speech is not heard (New International Version). Yet other translations put it that there is neither speech nor words; their voice is not heard (the New American Standard Bible, for one).

The second third of the Psalm (vv. 7–13) further clarifies the issue. The language shifts from ambiguity to unequivocality. Whatever the creation says, the creator who is the Word speaks differently and with startling clarity:

> The law of the Lord is perfect,
> reviving the soul.
> The statues of the Lord are trustworthy,
> making wise the simple.
> The precepts of the Lord are right,
> giving joy to the heart. . . .
> The ordinances of the Lord are sure
> and altogether righteous.
> They are more precious than gold;
> they are sweeter than honey. (NIV)

There is no doubt about the meaning of these verses. The speech of God through the law is undeniably clear. The handiwork, with its own peculiar glory is, *by contrast*, dumb, or at most ambiguous.[2] The lesson is obvious. If we desire to know what the maker is like and what he has to say; if we wish to be changed, we must turn from the handiwork to the maker, himself, listening to him speak in no uncertain terms. We can reduce the foregoing to a principle: *God's creation, as magnificent as it is, can at most point to the one who is the truth; truth alone converts and sets free.* God's handiwork does not possess the qualities and propositional accuracies of truth. Therefore it cannot articulate moral direction.[3]

Here is a second principle: *In the separation of revelation and creation, God has provided a clear opportunity for, and a clear distinction between, absolutes (revealed truth) and relativities (the wordless/deedless creation and its counterpart in human handiwork).* Each is a separate domain; each is entirely right; and the one should not be confused with the other. Revealed truth is fixed. It is eternal. Handiwork has no fixed reference point within itself. It will pass away.

Now if all of this is true of the incredibly variegated splendor of God's handiwork, it should be no less true of ours. Artwork after artwork utters speech; there is knowledge of a kind; it may be heard far and wide. But the speech of the artwork is not the same as the speech of the artist. This is just another way of saying that revelation is not the creation, the Creator is not the creation, and the music maker is not the music. If we want to know who the musician really is and what he or she believes, we should go to him or her to observe and listen. The music cannot tell us, even if the music maker wants it to; it is limited to declaring itself and pointing to its maker.

When we assume that certain kinds of art, and all of music, proclaim truth, truth itself is diffused. When we assume that beauty can proclaim truth, the result is often slick, obvious, gimmicky, and caricatured.[4] This is why so much of today's "witness art," including a lot of the worded/deeded kind, just does not work. In the rush to make the message clear, aesthetic qualities become blunted or compromised. Or if the aesthetic process is emphasized, the truth message, to the frustration of those who want immediate results, cannot be that easily formulated.

None of the foregoing is meant to imply that even though certain art forms may be amoral, their makers are not morally accountable. All artists are morally responsible for everything they do. While the *what* of art and music is in the domain of the relative, the *why* is always in the domain of moral accountability, under full scrutiny of the truth. God examines the intent of the heart before scrutinizing—as trite as this may sound—the content of the art. An exemplary Christian may make average art, and a moral libertine, great art. Yet the Christian will not fall and the libertine has no hope. In all cases, personal rectitude supersedes and is separate from handiwork. Furthermore, this concept of artifactual relativity is not to be confused with a standardless approach to making art and music. All true artists are, by nature, careful about the quality of their work. Integrity is always of the essence. But this integrity is not to be equated with moral or ethical integrity. It is an integrity of artistic wholeness, completeness, procedural excellence, and aesthetic rightness.

Creativity, Handiwork, and Idolatry

The Scriptures not only articulate a distinction between truth and handiwork, they denounce any linkage between the two. Such a linkage is idolatry. When we commit idolatry we abuse our creative gifts in the most flagrant way by fabricating concrete connections between what we believe and what we make. In an insidious way, beauty and "truth" are reunited and handiwork takes on causality. The very ones whom God created to be in dominion over creation fall under the spell and domain of a lesser creature, thinking it to be a greater creature. The shaper is thus shaped by what she or he has shaped.

As artists and music makers, we must avoid the assumption that something made can be allowed to switch its role from handiwork *under* dominion to handiwork *having* dominion, assuming prerogatives it does not inherently possess. "Pure" idolatry is the ultimate linkage of belief and artifact, as well as the ultimate reversal of cause and effect. Incipient idolatry comes from the idea that art and music possess the capability, by their presence and use, to shape behaviors.

When people say that rhythms, chords, or textures cause sexual license, violence, or drug abuse; whenever anybody—missionary or tribal person—says that certain kinds of music or rhythmic types are satanic, they are caught up in the same dilemma that Isaiah speaks of (chapter 44). There is really no difference between someone carving a god out of what otherwise is a piece of firewood and someone else who happens upon or makes a certain kind of music, expecting it to govern the actions of those hearing and using it.

These principles extend to the use of organ preludes, statuary, religious paintings, and architecture. They serve as warnings to anybody whose avowed intention is to use the arts as behavior modifiers in worship, entertainment, home, or office. They apply to any circumstance in which familiarity, repetition, and imputed meaning are used cumulatively and manipulatively. And they apply whenever anyone says that the presence of God is felt more keenly when music is made than when it is not.

The apostle Paul confronts this issue head-on when he says that idols are nothing (1 Corinthians 8:4). And Jeremiah states the same thing even more pungently (10:5):

> Like a scarecrow in a cucumber field are they,
> And they cannot speak. . . .
> Do not fear them,
> For they can do no harm,
> Nor can they do any good. (NASB)

Paul in particular is writing to bring freedom to those who had long assumed that this kind of handiwork had power of such magnitude that even the meat (another kind of handiwork) offered to them partook of the same causal powers that the idol did. Paul knew that the grip that idols had over the new Christians would not easily be broken, so he gave temporary instructions: to abstain from eating such meat until the sensitive Christians were spiritually mature enough to understand that they had been bound by an absolute lie concerning the power of handiwork. Paul's words that idols were nothing were not words that denied their material existence or even their value as handiwork. He did not mean that the handiwork itself was completely meaningless, but that it had absolutely no meaning or substance *as a god or as a causal agent*. Paul's worldview was so thorough that, once we fully grasp it, we can understand that when idols are stripped of their pretended meaning and power, they can still possess intrinsic, even aesthetic, worth. This is why idols can be considered art pieces, along with music, statuary, paintings, and architecture. In and of themselves, they can serve as examples of the stunning ability of people everywhere to imagine and craft, even when lost in the darkness of the Fall. In principle, what Paul, Isaiah, and Jeremiah were saying was that handiwork, idols included, cannot be allowed prerogatives outside their domain of existence as mere handiwork. Once they are, they become idols, whether they were originally intended to be or not.

So we can conclude that idolatry can be at work in two kinds of people: those whose worldview is dominated by the idea that handiwork can be consciously created to hold dominion over them; and those whose worldview is a mixture of opposing beliefs—this is called syncretism—so that while they may be committed to God through Christ, they still make room for the shaping power of handiwork. *However, Christians, freed from untoward assumptions about what art is and how it means, can actually see, feel, and hear more intensely; they can celebrate all the more riotously, simply because there is no confusion of messages, no false assumptions about causality, no worry about aberrant power and perverse behavioral leverage.* They can maintain complete freedom *from* the artwork, while being completely free to act *with* it. Faith rules over works, maker over handiwork, revelation over creation, and Creator over all. It is God who is both means and end, alpha and omega, author and finisher. Knowing this and living it out rescues both us and our art from error, misuse, and, above all, idolatry.

Why Non-Christians Can Make Beautiful and Useful Music

There are many people in the world and many kinds of music. Music from Papua New Guinea, from Nigeria, China, Singapore, Bali, Philadelphia, and Scotland. Music by atheists, Buddhists, Christians, agnostics, nihilists, and capitalists. Music like rap, jazz, gamelan, opera, bluegrass, rock, and classical. Music past, present, and future; improvised, composed; sold, given away, begged, borrowed, or stolen.

If we divide the world into two kinds of people, Christians and non-Christians, does this similarly mean two kinds of music and art? We have already learned that the music maker is not the music. If music and art cannot be one with their makers, can they be shaped to reflect what their makers believe? If Satan could create a maple tree, would it have to reflect Satan's mind—what Satan believes? Would it have to look different than God's maple tree? By extension, how can a non-Christian make anything but non-Christian music? And if so, how can a Christian make honest use of it?

The spotlight, for the last few decades, has been on the many kinds of rock music that Christians have decided to use. Preachers, evangelists, pamphleteers, seminar leaders, authors, and concerned parents are in a circular fuss over this issue. And now there is a new one: New Age music. Christians are being told that they should neither listen to this music nor use it. But some are doing both. Are they right or wrong? Is New Age a danger that was never quite reached with rock? And is rock a danger not quite reached by jazz? And so on.

Putting it the other way around, if the gospel is what it says it is; if it claims to make a new creation out of every one who turns to Christ; if it is claimed that Christians think and act differently than they did in their previous state; if thinking and acting differently means giving up many former practices that, as some purport, include certain art forms, does it not follow that there must be special ways of showing their regeneracy, not just by words of testimony, but by art itself? Should not special grace—the saving, renewing power of God—carve out such new territory that, in addition to Christian art, there should be Christian economics, Christian automobile designs, and Christian cuisine?

Fortunately, God is wiser than this. Even though God hates sin and longs for the whole world to come to repentance, he continues to anoint the creation and its inhabitants in numberless ways in spite of our fallenness. God blesses, refreshes, gifts, and enables the entire race. Theologians have termed this way of blessing *common grace*. It is a most refreshing doctrine. It explains why sinful people—morally ugly people—are given rain for their crops right along with righteous people. Common grace holds that God, in unmerited and unmeasured graciousness, brings gifts and provision to the whole of a world that is fallen and generally in rebellion. Common grace enables unregenerate people to perform noble deeds; to express strong societal, friendly, familial, and sexual love; to submit themselves to and show understanding for moral and ethical codes of behavior; and in the areas of technology, crafting, and the arts, to make beautiful, useful, and lasting artifacts.

Those who attack secular forms of music and art often overlook this principle. Instead they mix in arguments about lifestyles and lyrics. They introduce arguments about biological changes that certain kinds of music introduce—changes in pulse rates, blood pressure, and the like. They forget that during the course of every day, our biological systems are in constant flux. Beethoven changes us, the stock market does, digesting food does, exercising does, lullabies do, pep band music does, chocolate does, and so do reading books and wrestling with theological truths. But biological changes are not the same as moral changes, nor can they be said to cause them.

There is nothing un- or anti-Christian about any kind of music. By the same token, there is no such thing as Christian music. If there were, what would it be? Would it be the long-standing musical vocabularies of the church? If so, could it be argued that these flow from a pure stream of Christian influence all the way back to the early church? We know that this is not true because the music of the Western church represents a steady confluence of musical practices from all ethnic and cultural quarters, secular and churchly. Would it be from China? From New Guinea? Indonesia? How could it be when these nations made music before they heard of Christ? Even if it could be argued that there might be such a thing as Western Christian music, what do we do when we evangelize? Do we use this music? Is our music so indigenously Christian that we can honestly say that it should become the Christian music for the whole world?

If so, what should it be—Bach, Handel, Penderecki, Andre Crouch, Amy Grant, or Take Six? Many relevance-minded people would opt for Crouch or Grant, because that's what most contemporary Christians naturally choose. Others would say Bach or Penderecki because this kind of music is what contemporary Christians should be taught to choose. But what right do they have to say what somebody else should like? Besides, how can popular music really be Christian when it is "tainted" by its identity with secular pop music, or classical music when it is so "out of tune with the times"?

There is no scriptural way to answer these questions other than to say, right at the outset, that the doctrine of common grace helps us understand why all music, flowing out of the creativities of a thousand cultures, subcultures, lifestyles, and belief systems, can be good. And from within these, all good music should be offered to a Creator for whom a thousand tongues will never suffice.

The Relation Between Musical Content and Musical Context

Even though the foregoing has been argued from biblical and theological perspectives, it does not mean that everybody's problems will come to an end. What about the young man who could not break away from the near horror of hearing Bach in church? What about others whose experiences with many of today's musical styles have a similar effect on them, once they come to Christ? What about returning missionaries and their stories of the connections between demonic worship and musical style? We simply cannot throw theology at them and hope for the best. We've been warned about this kind of behavior in the book of James (2:15–16). It really does no good if we create a musical version of this passage and say, "Go in peace, be delivered; all music is okay and so are you."

We must now examine the reasons why music is morally neutral, yet seemingly capable of carrying strong or shifting moral messages, and why we are morally accountable for all the music we choose, even though music is morally neutral. Here are three concepts that can be brought to bear on this issue.

1. *Music has no interior beacon that guarantees permanent meaning. Unlike truth, which is transcultural, absolute, and unchangeable, music can shift in meaning from place to place and time to time.* Of all the art forms, music is inherently the most flexible. The music of Bach, as deeply fixed within the churchly contexts of his time and ours, can still shift meanings while remaining great music in its own right. For Lutherans it is church music, *par excellence.* For the young convert from Satanism, it was evil. In its original form, the tune "Austria" was the imperial national anthem, "Gott erhalte Franz den Kaiser," composed by Haydn. He then used it as the principal theme for the slow movement in his Emperor Quartet. In this guise it reflects the essentially secular contexts for which it was written and is perfectly at home in the concert hall. It is also the tune for "Deutschland über Alles," the German national anthem. And for Jewish people, it is associated with the unspeakable horrors of the holocaust. And finally, it is the tune to which the hymn "Glorious Things of Thee Are Spoken" is sung in virtually all American churches. To American Christians this tune's primary meaning is "sacred." To them, it carries virtually none of its first two meanings, unless one or the other was impressed first into their memories. There is no way to explain this phenomenon other than that music, as music, is completely relative.

2. The foregoing can be stated as a behavioral principle: *Even though music is wordless and deedless, the people making it and the contexts in which it is made are not. The more a piece of music is repeated in the same context, the more it will begin to "mean" that context.* Music is the most context friendly of all the arts. It attaches itself quickly, spongelike, to whatever surrounds it. And by repetition, it is eventually perceived to equate with the context. Through its expressive power, it draws the context up into itself to the extent that the meaning, *originally generated by the context itself*, appears to come directly from within the music. What was originally extrinsic and referential—from the outside—gradually moves from the

outside to the inside and now appears to be generated by the musical content itself. By contrast, worded and deeded art forms are context informing. They speak *directly* to a context directly out of their own propositional mechanisms. The Word of God is not context absorbing; it is context disturbing. It does not change with the context. Rather, the context must change because of its presence.

There is no other explanation for music "becoming" sacred or secular, good and evil. This is how we can explain that an art piece—say a drinking song or a pagan symbol—can be gradually adapted to churchly use. It explains why people who consider music to be organically linked to the activities of everyday life also consider it to be inseparable from their belief systems. It is these linkages between belief and handiwork that produce false assumptions about the causal power of handiwork. In the case of the early Christians, meat offered to idols was a profound part of the linkage to the non-Christian world. As we have seen, these Christians were warned away from it until they were spiritually strong enough to see the artificiality of the linkage. This being accomplished, they could do the disengaging and see meat for what it was—nourishment—and the idol for what it was—nothing. And what is true of meat and idols can be equally true of music.

When somebody says that Christian music is Christian by virtue of a particular kind of content, he or she commits the same error as the secular and pagan thinkers who have found a way to impute moral and ethical qualities to an art form—to mere handiwork. This kind of thinking is in "idol territory," and whenever it appears, it confuses and divides. It is contrary to every biblical and creational doctrine there is. It is contrary to the doctrine of common grace. It divides truth and absolutizes relativity. It creates false hierarchies and, among young people, creates undue confusion and induces deep fear, especially when comments are made by well-meaning but theologically uninformed Christian leaders who link satanism up with the musical content of rock. This has led, in some instances, to deep emotional upset and fear. Then the error is doubled when they point to the fear and upset as concrete evidence of the evil nature of the music against which the young people have been warned. Lacking proper biblical insight, they seem unable to say that rock, as with idols, is nothing—mere handiwork. They do not understand the collateral principle of the weakened conscience—that conscience caused by associative memories. Instead they impute intrinsic power to the artifact and then proceed to build fear upon error.

3. *There is a difference between being moved by music and being morally directed or changed by it.* Everybody knows that music moves people emotionally. This being so, it is up to each individual and within each person's power to decide what moral actions can be taken or refused when music is heard. For instance, when I hear a march, I might be emotionally moved to move my feet. But I still must make a moral decision as to whether I march for war or for peace. Or if I like to dance I must make a moral decision as to what dancing means to me in the face of being emotionally moved both by music and dancing. The music cannot do this for me, although sometimes I would like to think that it can.

Those who condemn or praise music because of what it *makes* people do have it all backward or upside down. They overlook Jesus' words in Mark 7:15: "Nothing outside a man can make him 'unclean' by going into him. Rather, it is what comes out of a man that makes him 'unclean'" (NIV). In other words, people behave exactly the way they want to, down deep in their hearts. And then, in the contextual union of music and circumstance, they continue to behave the way they were behaving before they heard the music. In fact, they join and identify with a context because it accords with the lifestyle that they are free to choose or reject. In their blindness, they will blame or praise the context for the behavior that issues out of the entire affair. Whereas some might say that rock 'n' roll leads some people into sexual sin or drug abuse, the more scriptural principle would be stated as follows: Those who already have it in their hearts to sin sexually or abuse themselves will listen to rock 'n' roll. They will then link the music, its emotional impact, and the larger environment to their worldview and behave accordingly.

This error can just as easily be carried over into Christian worship, when we say that a certain kind of music causes us to worship. The same scriptural principles that apply to rock 'n' roll and misbehavior must be applied here as well. Those who truly *want* to worship, *as an ongoing condition of the heart*, should not credit music with the power to bring worship about. They will worship irrespective of music.

It is just as wrong to assume that music causes worship as it is to say that it causes sexual behavior. In this sense one can speak of contextual addictions to music, a state not unlike addiction to chemical substances. Even though it is socially more benign, contextual addiction might be as spiritually damaging. We might go so far as to say that, on a given Sunday morning, some handiwork-dependent Christians "shoot up" with music—getting some kind of high or fix—in exactly the same way as those who use needles and pills in other circumstances. In short, it is not what music does to us, it is what we choose to do with music, by virtue of the condition of our heart.

Artistic Relativity, Christian Freedom, and Accountability

Even though Christians are potentially the most free to understand the subtle differences between absolutes and relativities, content and context, some still find themselves unable to use certain kinds of music for reasons of conscience. Although they may theologically or intellectually understand that music is incapable of moral causality, they still cannot break free of the hold it may have over them. Powers of association are especially hard to overcome, especially if they have developed over a long period of time and/or have grown out of especially intense experiences and personal commitments. Sensitive Christians may find themselves in exactly the same position as their earlier brothers and sisters who considered meat offered to idols unfit to eat. So we go back to Paul's instructions (Romans 14; 1 Corinthians 8) and apply them to musical practice.

These principles are simple yet far-reaching. Their importance lies not only in the separation of relativities and absolutes but in the distinction between obedience to relativities *through discernment* and obedience to absolutes *by commandment*. Here's how the principles work. First, obedience through discernment does not apply to absolutes. I would be foolish to ask the Lord to give me discernment as to whether to lust or not. When it comes to matters of morality, I must directly obey. And if I pray, it is for the strength to obey. On the other hand, if I am to make a choice between two good things—whether to become a doctor or a mechanic—or among things that are morally relative—rock or Bach—I pray for discernment. I must then take one of two actions. I use the music through a new strength and freedom of conscience, or I abstain out of conscience until I find release. If release does not come, my abstinence continues. *In either case, I experience true freedom.*

This next point is crucial. *Decisions like this must always be personal, not corporate.* They must be based on what the individual believer is personally free to do or not do, not on what the group is about to do. If it is wrong for me to listen to reggae, Bach, New Age, Tibetan chant, or rock, then I must, in complete freedom, abstain even while others freely engage. And it would be just as wrong for me to say that any of these musics are wrong for anybody else.

How do I discern? This timeworn adage is still useful: If I have real doubt, I must abstain. This parallels Paul's statement that whatsoever is not of faith is sin. The reverse is just as true: Whatsoever *is* of faith is righteousness. Taken together, these two statements form the Christian's personal creed for living among, and using, relativities. If faith is the only thing the just can live by—a perfectly legitimate rewording of Habakkuk 2:4—and if one's life is to be an uninterrupted flow of acts of worship, then all musical choice and action must be by faith—personal faith, not someone else's. Otherwise, I must avoid whatever offends me until I can freely offer it up. In the meantime I have three responsibilities: (1) I must continue to make offerings out of the remainder of the thousand tongues with which I do have freedom; (2) I must continue to pray for the freedom to break old associations and erroneous teaching; (3) I must trust the Spirit of Christ in others who are free to enjoy what I am not yet able to.

All of this reduces down to this simple test: Can I offer all my music and art directly to Christ as a part of my personal life of holiness? If I can, he will accept it; if I can't, he won't. It's that simple, whether the offering is a twelve-bar blues or a hymn tune. The Christian is free of the moral nothingness of music exactly the same way a former idolater is released from the nothingness of the idol. In all cases, each Christian is bound to the weight of, and freed by, truth itself.

Only Christians have this freedom. Only the Christian gospel offers this gracious provision of personal initiative, personal responsibility, and personal decisiveness. Christian artists and musicians can rest in the knowledge that as long as their hearts are hungry after God and the righteousness of the Kingdom, they can move freely and discerningly among the wealth of art forms and musics, deciding by faith, erring here, and triumphing there, but always by faith—faith unto faith. God will protect, instruct, guide, and cleanse. God will not forsake, scoff, or run off. God is just as interested in the spiritual quests of the artistically gifted as in the ministries of a Bible translator.

These spiritual isometrics—striving for while striving against—are bound to bring breadth, width, and fullness to each person. We must be free to challenge doubt with faith and challenge faith with even more faith. Christ will be sure to win. In Isaiah's words, our Savior will never extinguish the dimly burning wick of the fearful and sensitive (Isaiah 42:3). He always stoops to free and correct.

One final thought. Christians can ruin the concept of discerning freedom through a form of legalism. We already know of one kind—trying to prove our righteousness by what we do *not* do. The second kind is equally dangerous and quite subtle. This is where we prove how free we are by what we *do* do. In order to show our freedom, we perform, watch, or listen without attending to matters of conscience. We blithely talk about everything being worship and freedom without examining the deeper reasons that drive all thought and action. Every Christian must pray for personal discernment, both in order to make personal choices and to avoid imitating anybody else's. Paraphrasing the Apostle Paul's words in Romans 14:23, whatsoever is from somebody else's faith may turn out to be sin for me.

NOTES

1. It is necessary to divide the arts up into two kinds: those that contain words, deeds, or a mixing of them, and those that do not. This division is crucial, for it is through words and deeds that moral content is most easily shown. (See also note 3.) Consequently, worded-deeded art forms are bound more closely to moral content and response than others. The first category comprises most of literature, drama, cinema, photography, theater, dance, mime, and certain kinds of visual art. Virtually all music falls into the last category, as do certain kinds of literature and visual art and photography.

   While music combines easily with all other art forms, its combination with words can be particularly troublesome. Moral judgments are often passed on music when, in fact, they should be directed toward the words sung to it. Music is intrinsically the most abstract of all the arts, not in the sense that visual art can be abstract, but in the sense that its referential mechanisms—its ways of referring to contexts outside itself—are more ambiguous and variable than in any other art form.

2. Since the Romans and Psalms passage say that the creation declares something, we can conclude that it says something similar to this: "I have been created; I have a glory of a certain kind, and in a mysterious way I proclaim the existence of my Creator, but I cannot speak in place of Him. I can only point to His infinitely greater person and glory. Those who look to me for moral direction or assume that by listening to me they will be converted are turning from the Creator to the creature. Go to the Creator for truth. Look to the Creator and be saved."

3. Propositional truth can only be communicated by means of words and then deeds. This is why we have both the Scriptures—God's Word to us—and the incarnate Son of God, the only person ever capable of a perfect oneness between word and deed. We need the Word first, because it gives us knowledge of the exceeding sinfulness of sin, the mysteries of godliness, the way to salvation, and all necessary direction for faith and practice. Above all, we need the Savior, to whom the Word points and fully discloses, and in whom all of the treasures of God's wisdom and knowledge are hidden (Colossians 2:3).

   Christianity has the edge on all other belief systems because of the wholeness and grandeur of the doctrine of an all-revealing God who is truth and whose Son is the incarnate Word. The God who speaks is not only the God who speaks and it is so; the one who speaks is also the one who can reduce his speech to the dimensions of human language without diminishing the value and fullness of the revelation. Thus when God speaks in the Scriptures and through the Son, God reveals—shares—his own personhood and speech. Those who hear and do the Word of God directly share in the person, work, speech, and action of God. They in turn become deeded word bearers or living epistles.

The act of revelation is from infinite to finite, from God's transcendent speech to human language. In the process, truth does not change its content. It certainly changes modes (infinite speech to human speech), but in all of this truth does not become less than God's Word any more than the Son of God became less than God when he took flesh upon himself. It is in this sense that an exact parallel may be made between the kenosis, or emptying, that the Son of God undertook and what happened to the speech of God when it became enscriptured. In both cases, infinity is not robbed. Simply, though mysteriously, it is emptied. The emptied Word of God is no less the Word of God than the emptied Christ is less than the person of God. In this respect, the correctness of our Christology and bibliology must be tested against each other.

The power and importance of words, deeds, and deeded words lie in the foregoing principles. The arts can never fully rise to these prerogatives, nor need we feel loss if they cannot. They still rise to great occasion, just as the creation itself does. Anything that can proclaim the glory of the Creator; any humanly made thing that can point to its own maker, fallen or redeemed; anything that can do these has extraordinary worth. But having extraordinary worth is not the same as having infinite worth.

4. These remarks are not meant to condemn the use of art and music in Christian witness, but to distinguish between art *in* witness and art *as* witness. This subject will be discussed more fully in chapter 10.

Chapter 3

MUSICAL PLURALISM AND DIVERSITY

Son, whatever you do in life, don't take anybody's song away.
— MY FATHER TO ME, WHEN I WAS ABOUT TEN

All music is folk music. I ain't never heard no horse sing.
— BIG BILL BROONZY

Webster's definition of pluralism is as follows:

a. The state of society in which members of diverse ethnic, racial, religious, or social groups maintain an autonomous participation in and development of their traditional culture or special interest within the confines of a common civilization.
b. A concept, doctrine, or policy advocating this state.

I have constructed another definition that remains true to the intent of the above, while taking better account of contemporary American society and its diverse musical practices.

a. In a population located within a democracy, pluralism is the presence, coexistence, equality, and possible interrelationship of different types;
b. In any segment of that population, pluralism means recognizing, engaging in, rearranging, or adding to any number of these types, as informed by the values and larger practices of that segment.

There is more music today than ever before, and each of us has unprecedented access to all of it. First, music is accumulating historically. As time passes, the amount of music naturally keeps increasing. Second, music is accumulating horizontally. As more contemporary musicians rub creative shoulders, constant evolution takes place; styles widen, they are transformed and paraphrased. This means an enormous multiplying of styles, fusions, and transmutations. The ease with which musicians can know what others are creating grows with each technological advance. Music is everywhere; no commercial enterprise is without it; virtually no religious exercise is without it; no home is without it; no restaurant, no car dealership, no supermarket. We even have to put up with it on the telephone while we wait for a party to answer. And all of this means more composers, arrangers, performers, improvisers, and technology; more sounds, colors, textures and experiments, and styles.

Third, the global scope of music is being noticed and used as never before. Ethnomusicologists, using state-of-the-art recording equipment, are literally creating a worldwide musical archive. And it is ours for the asking. The influences of world music on current Western musical practices are more pervasive than at any other time in our musical history. They cover every aspect of music making: instrumentation, timbre, texture, melody, rhythm, instrumental and vocal styles—classical through popular. In the same way, American popular music, especially rock (by all odds the most influential music of our time), has made inroads into the music of other cultures. It is not uncommon to hear Korean rock, Chinese rock, Hispanic rock, and the like. Each uses the overall rock style while containing a rather pronounced musical "accent"; the ethnicity hangs on despite the influences. Much of this ethnic rock music is in transition. As to whether the ethnic roots will win out and somehow transform rock or rock will win and subsume ethnicity remains to be seen.

Within this huge array of worldwide music making, the church is arguably the most musically diverse body in human history. Over its chronological life and throughout its nearly numberless multicultural practices, it has thought up, borrowed, imitated, stolen, adapted, and paraphrased more kinds of music than any other collection of people. Presently, there are two forces at work. Through the music of mass electronic evangelism and traveling musical witness groups, a popular westernized style is increasingly heard worldwide. Meanwhile, a newfound interest in the indigenous church is stimulating efforts to create music for worship and witness that grows directly out of the musical roots of a given culture itself.

Given these layers and tensions, could it be argued that musical diversity is part of the leftovers from the Tower of Babel? Is diversity a sign that we have not yet found the right music, or, if it already exists, how do we find a way to spread its good news? On the Christian side, while we pray and work for a whole world turned to the same Christ, why should we not work for the development of a single, worldwide, Christian music? Wouldn't it be wonderful if the whole world could band together into one huge congregation and sing the same hymns? Since more and more Christians everywhere seem to be picking up on "How Great Thou Art," "Amazing Grace," "Jesus Loves Me," "Majesty," and "All Hail the Power," is this not a sign that some such universality might already be in progress? What about the way people deep in New Guinea and high up in Switzerland all seem to pick up so easily on rock music? Is it our next task to begin to distill the musics of the world down into some rich broth, as natural and nurturing as the very air we commonly breathe?

The Creation as a Model for Pluralism: A Summary

We should cherish diversity because God does. God not only imagines and creates with endless variety, God calls good everything in the creation. Everything has its uniqueness, its place, its meaning, usefulness, and its interdependence. Thus unity and diversity are aspects of each other.

There are many layers of diversity in the creation. First, there are discreet kinds of handiwork: butterflies, avocados, Gila monsters, monkeys, galaxies, and sea horses. Second, there are numerous species within kinds. Furthermore, diversity continues almost endlessly within a single species, for no two oak trees are alike.

Some things are more beautiful, more complex, or more advanced than others, but this fact does not undo the principle of completeness and integrity with which each thing is made. Thus while some things may be said to be more beautiful, more useful, or more advanced than others, this does not mean that the lesser things have no right to exist or in God's view are unworthy. God notes every sparrow's fall and numbers every hair on our heads.

Just as there are numberless species and subspecies of tree, so there are of music; just as certain trees thrive in a given environment, so with music; just as certain environments may welcome many species at once, so with music; just as one person may consider one species of tree more aesthetically pleasing or functionally useful than another, so with music. In the meantime, the intrinsic worth of every type, along with its contextual ability to be useful, is common to all musics as it is to all trees.

What Pentecost Tells Us About Pluralism

The astonishing events that took place fifty days after Jesus' resurrection during a time-honored Jewish holy day are not only history, but also a parable. The history is carefully laid out in Acts 2. Through a directly manifest visitation of the Holy Spirit, a group of believers was enabled to speak in a bewildering assortment of tongues. They were overheard by a conglomerate "from every nation under heaven" (verse 5) as they spoke in the assorted languages of the conglomerate. After that, Peter preached a powerful evangelistic sermon that was understandable in every language group represented. Tongues were loosened, ears were unstopped, and hearts were turned. A union unprecedented in the history of salvation was brought to hearing and proclamation. In a profound sense, Pentecost is Babel turned right side up: all speech is unified because it is God, no longer people, who is building toward the heavens.

The story of Pentecost goes further than its historical reality. It is also a parable that urges us into the knowledge that the gospel is comfortable in any culture and its message finds easy residence in the languages, cultural ways, and thought styles (but not thought systems) of countless societies. *In other words, whoever seeks to move a culture towards transformation by Christ must join it, participating in the transformation from within.*

God is not Western; God is not Eastern; God is not exclusively the God of classical culture or of primitive culture; God is the Lord of the plethora, the God of the diverse, the redeemer of the plural. Likewise, God calls for response in different languages, dialects, and idioms, accepting them through the Son. Pentecost tells us that one artistic tongue is only a start and a thousand will never suffice. There is no single chosen language or artistic or musical style that, better than all others, can capture and repeat back the fullness of the glory of God. One culture has capabilities, nuances, and creative ways that others simply do not possess. This truism cannot be avoided. Cultures are not infinite. No single one can hold the wholeness of praise and worship or the fullness of the counsel of God.

Thus God does not want to hear only Beethoven and Ken Medema or see just Renoirs, Vermeers, and Wyeths. God does not want to be limited to Christian rap or Pakistani chant. God wants to hear the whole world in its countless tongues and amazingly diverse musics making praise after praise. God accepts not only the offerings of a highly trained choir, but also the song of the arrow maker in Brazil. Furthermore, with more patience than we can imagine, God awaits entirely new songs sung for the first time from a tribe in Cambodia, a Mexican *barrio*, and a Scottish hamlet.

But the idea that God awaits and welcomes the countless kinds of music is not enough all by itself. The parable continues. Pentecost tells us that each of us must live *pentecostally*—in the spirit of Pentecost—among the musics of the world. Living pentecostally does not imply a change of denomination or worship style; it means that we strive to seek out and welcome a variety of musics to our own lives, even as Jesus welcomes them into his Kingdom. Living pentecostally means that each of us, as much as

possible, should revel in the whole world of musical creativity—
transculturally, transstylistically, and transhistorically. Since no one
culture can "say it all," how fitting it is for Christians to want to join
the creative ways of other cultures, if for no other reason than to fill
out their praise!

Musical pentecost is not one music pitted against another. It is a
sharing, a commingling, a co-celebration, a co-usage among many
tongues. Artistic pentecost is community. It unifies. It brings the
bagpipes of Scotland into union with the balalaikas of Russia; it
tunes the nose flute of Papua New Guinea to the marimbas of
Guatemala and joins the Jesus rap of the inner city to intercourse
with the gamelan of Bali. Where the Spirit is there is unity. When
the Spirit authors the languages of praise there is communion.
Where the Spirit of the Lord is there is liberty. The thousand
tongues become common song, and the body of Christ, in all of its
parts, freely joins in singing "alleluia." Consequently, musical community, analogous to the apostle Paul's concept of the oneness of
the body, does not consist in the importance of jazz *over* folk *over*
rock. Each part needs the other, and all parts—even the "unseemly"
ones—have something important to do and contribute. Each part
needs and is influenced by others; each has some kind of value and
usefulness for someone in the community; and each is subject to
the pursuit of excellence.

Musical pluralism does not begin with aesthetics but with people.
No matter how favorable or objectionable their music might be at
first blush, it is of primary importance to understand that the music
makers are honest-to-goodness people who must be loved first of all
as such. The next step is to understand that they honestly love the
music they make or they would not have made it to begin with.
Following on this, faith is to be exercised—not saving faith, but
trust in the worth and teachability of the image of God in each
individual, no matter how different, botched, or hidden it might be.
In the meantime, while we teach, we learn because we are
encountering the remarkable ability of different people to imagine
and craft musics of which we ourselves are initially—or even

continually—incapable. Teaching and correcting while learning are risky; sometimes these exercises can stymie or even offend us, but they are entirely necessary.

Pluralism and the Nature of Human Inquiry

All true learning requires that inquiry be made into multiple options. Dedicated teachers and students regularly make it a habit to study, compare, and critique matters that go beyond the usual, even those that may not be personally palatable. This is preferable to teaching and learning what is already believed in, known, or personally pleasurable while ignoring, not tolerating, or even ridiculing the opposites. True teaching and learning do not properly take place until alternatives are thoroughly looked into and understood.

The discovery of new and unfamiliar musical ways may not always be pleasant if we have limited ourselves to the idea that what we already know is all that we need or if we believe that music is meant only to bring a thoughtless kind of pleasure. But choices cannot be made without exploring options, and even though no one is expected to choose everything they explore, choices themselves can never be generated in the abstract. This means that teachers must be more practitionally pluralistic than the students whom they are attempting to teach. Music education, then, is less an imparting of love for music than a stretching and reforming of a love that already exists.

We do not become pluralist merely by intellectually recognizing and theoretically justifying pluralism. We have to *do* pluralism. The first thing we must do is to move from hearing music to listening to it. Our culture is so full of music that, in a profound way, it has become empty of it. In a period of, say, a media-filled week, all of us will "hear" Muzak, adult contemporary, classic rock, classical, jazz, swing, rag, blues, Broadway, hard rock, soft rock, straight rock, jazz-rock fusions, rhythm and blues, house music, hip hop, rap, country, gospel, Christian contemporary, New Age, bluegrass, hymns, Scripture and praise songs, anthems, ethnic, and folk. Within these, some kind or kinds of music will form a center, from which active excursions into other musics can be made. These excursions, marked by a progression from hearing to listening, will determine the extent to which we are becoming more pluralistic.

One way to go about deeper listening is through what we can call adjacent pluralism. Here is an example. If I like Broadway show tunes and I want to branch out from there, the stylistic similarities between them and certain kinds of classical music can take me into the music of Tchaikovsky, Gershwin, or Bernstein. Then as I get more into their music, especially that of Gershwin and Bernstein, I am being prepared for certain kinds of jazz. I might then take the jazz path and go historically backward into swing, ragtime, and blues; I could then move "sideways" into rhythm and blues, temporarily postponing the idea that Tchaikovsky could lead me over into Rachmaninoff and from there back into Brahms, Schumann, and Rachmaninoff; or instead of that, Rachmaninoff could take me, with a few jolts here and there, into the music of Prokofiev and Stravinsky, which in turn could lead me into ethnic Russian music or down into later twentieth-century classicism or neoclassicism or back into jazz.

There is another approach, through what we can call distant pluralism. The listener practicing distant pluralism simply ignores the stylistic adjacencies spoken of above and instead leapfrogs boundaries. Perceptual leaps are taken that are based less on the interconnectedness of musical types than on the sheer impact and/or exoticism of the new music. The listener may have few handles for understanding the music. Melodic and harmonic pitches (if there is melody or harmony as we know it) may sound "out of tune"; vocal qualities may appear to be distorted; instrumental timbre and color may be unlike anything we know; or there may appear to be a complete lack of structure, usual flow, or variation. Getting to know this music may take extraordinary trust and ear stretching. It always helps to remember that this music is quite natural for those who are making it. Through patient listening and contextualizing, the music becomes more and more familiar, more and more a part of one's normal perception. Whereas in adjacent pluralism, we can make connections more through the music itself, distant pluralism may take willpower and aggressiveness.

Pluralism, Centrism, and Prejudice

As stated above, all credible pluralists have a center—a musical and cultural locating point, a home. This then forms a perceptual base from which additional musical choices are made. Musical pluralism is not an ambiguous, sonic anarchy; it is not a trendy and valueless everything-is-okay-ism. Even though we are free to assume that all music possesses its own kind of worth, no one is obligated to assume that there is no intelligent choosing, no sorting out, and no hierarchy of values. Totally relativized pluralism, in which everything is considered the same, is an intellectual travesty. And yet, there is a vast difference between having a musical center and being musically prejudiced. Ethnocentrism is not the same as racial prejudice or discrimination. Ethnocentrism is simply the act and process of knowing, loving, and acting within and upon our own civilizational, cultural, and behavioral ways. Prejudice and banal pseudotolerance both deny the critical insights that should always accompany creative conscience. They neuter imagination, dull craftsmanship, and genericize uniqueness.

There is a new kind of prejudice taking place in the name of multicultural education. Some of its advocates insist that while we need to reach out to and study other cultures, we should question, if not reject, the study of Western culture, particularly its classical art pieces. They also make the mistake of limiting multicultural education to the study of a few select popular, ethnic, and folk traditions, while ignoring the study of classical traditions. They further err by forgetting that, with the exception of Asian and certain African populations, most of what they are really encouraging is still Western (as in the case of Hispanic music) or a mix of two originally disparate traditions (as in African American music). As a result, students are programmed into a pattern of thought that pits Western high culture—white, male, and racist—against the rest of the world's cultures. The next step is a very short one: prejudice reappears in the name of multiculturalism. Any attempt, therefore, to say anything about how music *x* might conceivably be better than music *y* would immediately be branded as racist or prejudicial. But prejudice—the real hard stuff—is different. It comes about when comments about quality and appropriateness are turned into the raising or lowering of the worth of the individual or the people responsible for who they are and what they have produced. It is at this point that preference turns into discrimination; education ceases and propaganda takes over. More than that, love for people and a sense of unity is completely displaced.

Centeredness—our sense of home and place—is the only legitimate context for pluralism. It works this way: If we genuinely love *ourselves*, culturally and ethnically, we will naturally love the ways of others. To love our own musical ways brings us the resilience, assurance, and freedom to look lovingly into the musical ways of others and even to be nurtured by them. This is simply the Golden Rule stated musically: If and as I truly love my immediate musical world, I will be able to understand the love of others for their ways.

Every serious pluralist should have three centers—better yet, a centeredness that is unified three ways.

1. *There must be a practitional center or centers.* The key word is *practitional*, which implies an active—as opposed to passive—engagement with a musical center or centers. For some, the center might be jazz; for others, Hispanic popular, Christian contemporary, or Western classical. The principle behind pluralism is that we expand our center carefully and integratively, refusing to be bound by the single dimensions of the single type with which we have begun. This includes growth within the type as well as from the type. There are too many kinds of classical music, for example, for anyone to assume that knowledge of Renaissance motets will

automatically produce a love for Stravinsky. Outward growth from our center can come about through the workings of adjacent pluralism and distant pluralism—better yet, an ongoing combination of the two.

2. *There must be a qualitative center.* In other words, as pluralism expands quantitively, concern for quality remains central. Whatever we do musically; however we explore new musics; no matter how much or little of each type we face, we must always seek the best. This might mean going through quite a bit of questionable music. But the best way to gain a sense of quality is to gradually experience and sense it—to sort it out from among the larger quantity. While risky, this is a far better way than to memorize the pronouncements or mimic the tastes and preferences of others. All the while, we must bear this in mind: The world of music is too large, too rich, too varied, to be confined only to greatness. While we must certainly cherish greatness, we must also cherish the simple goodness of music, along with the worth of the people who make it.

3. *There must be a biblical center.* That is, we should seek out biblical reasons that justify pluralism. While creation provides a visible justification, the story of Pentecost, both as history and metaphor, opens the door to biblical thought. These two provide a model for diversity, for unity within diversity, and open the way for a discussion of quality without prejudice.

Love, Unity, and Music Making: Brother and Sister Keeping

We have heard diatribes about bad music, poor taste, and mediocrity. Many of our musical choices, while made out of some kind of affection, have sometimes been met with scolding, as if choosing poor music were the same as breaking a window or cussing. It has caused a lot of people who naturally love music to worry that what they like might be considered by the "real artists" to be in bad taste. In fact, many of the "real artists" have the same worries. They have developed verbal mannerisms that they use to dance around the subject of quality: "Interesting" or "But what do you think?" or "It really depends, I suppose, on whether one really likes that particular style or not." In the face of all this, many people have simply lost that natural, childlike love for music and have substituted a kind of etiquette—stiff, condescending, separatist, reserved, mannered, or merely trendy. And not a few have ended up hating the very music that they have been unlovingly told to love. The sum of it all is that great music itself suffers because love—or whatever the feelings these devotees have—for music has all too often taken precedence over love for people.

Here are a few stories about different kinds of music making and makers, some good, some not so good, but each participating in a kind of loveliness.

Some time ago, my wife and I attended the wedding of one of our nephews in a small community in Wisconsin. The majority of the people in attendance were farmers—good, wholesome people. The men, most of them, had those square, strong hands that come of pulling and lifting. They walked as if most of the time they had been bending over things. The women showed a kind of beauty which can only come of sharing fundamental things: hard work, the uncertainties of nature, and the joy and hurt of family, home and community.

Of course all were dressed in their best Sunday clothes. The wedding party wore tuxes and formals. There was beauty here too—not the calculated and socially easy beauty of those who have special costumes for everything: work, aerobics, concerts, and dining out. This was the beauty of contrasts: the everyday and the special—square hands, bent backs, ruddy faces, tuxes, formal wear, a formal ceremony, and formal music. The beauty lay in the very awkwardness of doing special and unfamiliar things but doing them because it was right that they be done just that way.

Nor was the music the kind that they were used to doing. It was traditional, classical wedding music: Wagner, Mendelssohn, Malotte's "Lord's Prayer." The music was not particularly well done, by the standards of those who are better trained. But these people, as best they could, had reached into a sector of artistic creativity to which they were almost completely unused. There was a sweetness and a freshness to the music that moved me very deeply.

My two sons do not like classical music. Without being coercive, I've tried to show them why this music can be so beautiful and why I can be hooked on it while loving the kinds of music that they have so far limited themselves to. Both of them make music. My older son plays a pretty good blues harp, and my younger son, the electric guitar.

This younger son has accomplished something that at once frustrates me, moves me, and makes me proud. He has developed into a very good player of blues and classic rock, but especially the blues. He has done this with a determination and passion that I find lacking in many college music majors and church musicians.

He talked me one day into buying him a guitar. He took tapes of his idol Stevie Ray Vaughan up to his room and without knowing anything about guitars or music or how music works—refusing any kind of consistent study with a teacher—proceeded to try to play like Stevie, tape after tape, lick after lick. Hour after hour, day after day, week after week, he did this. As I overheard this I could only think of how little children learn to walk and talk. At first there are stumbles and babbles. But as time, repetition, experiment, and perseverance combine, the babble turns to intelligibility and intelligibility to articulateness—all without learning how to read or memorizing the rules of syntax and grammar.

So with this son of mine. All this time, he could only trust his ear. He still cannot read music and refuses to learn. This frustrates me. But the rest moves me—often to tearfulness—and makes me proud, this sojourn from cacophony to emerging finesse. I heard the whole struggle. He is not just my son, he is my musical brother—I with a doctorate in music and he with his own home-grown gutsiness. I only wish his tastes were as pluralistic as mine, so that we could love Bach and blues together. But that will come. Meantime, we're still brothers.

Awhile back, I went to Louisville, Kentucky, on some business. My wife accompanied me. While sightseeing, she happened upon the Louisville Folk Arts Festival. She came back to the hotel quite excited about what she saw and heard. She encouraged me to break away and take in as much of it as time would allow. I did. I saw folk artists, gunsmiths, quilters, painters, instrument and toy makers. I came upon a bluegrass band. I was transfixed with the wonderful music they made and the equally wonderful way they made it—no big fuss, just standing or sitting and quietly making the music. I was struck by a mixture of the commonplace and the special. Their elegance, peace, and integrity were like a benediction or a soothing ointment.

Several years ago, I was invited to the island of Tortola to run a three-week choral workshop and give organ lessons to those islanders whose training, up until then, had been virtually nonexistent. The three weeks' work culminated in a combination choral festival and organ recital. While many events and circumstances knit me to many people during that time, it was what happened during the recital that drew me as near to them as anything else. I was playing Bach's "Jesu, Joy of Man's Desiring." At the first entrance of the chorale tune itself, virtually the entire congregation spontaneously began humming the tune as it appeared, phrase by phrase. For these wonderful people, music making, even during a supposedly formal organ recital, was simply another way they—not just I—could join. So we made music together, as we did in the next selection, when they hummed and I played "O Sacred Head Now Wounded."

I know a pastor's wife who, in several churches, works also as the minister of music. Each of these churches has been quite small, with extremely modest musical and financial resources. She wanted to do a children's musical but had no money to purchase any music. So she proceeded to put something together herself, not by composing, which she could not do, but by compiling. The musical was about Jesus and his love, and she wanted to make his love for children as real as she could. What she did was powerful and creative. She took a little child, dressed her in a costume from biblical times, and had her sing these words:

> Jesus loves me! this I know,
> For I heard Him tell me so;
> Little ones to him belong. . . .

In my early years of college teaching, I had a part-time job as organist-choirmaster in a nearby church. The music program was a typical one: a junior choir and an adult choir, each singing regularly in the early and late service, respectively. The music was a fairly well balanced combination of hymns, gospel songs, and classical music.

There was one wrinkle in all of this, which in some churches would have been quickly "dealt with." But in Grace Conservative Baptist Church, Nanuet, New York, it was simply part of the communion of the saints, part of the love and unity of music making. During congregational singing, one person invariably whistled the tunes, stanza by stanza, week after week. It carried over all else, the organ included. But it was never challenged. For some reason, I didn't feel the need to protest, despite my ongoing training in the very highest of high art practices at Union Theological Seminary. For some strange reason, this whistling fit. There was something too honest and genuine and right about it. The singing, the whistling, and the organ playing were strangely of one cloth.

My great-grandmother lived to age 102. On her hundredth birthday we had a party for her. By this time she was in a nursing home, still quite physically strong but mentally weak. She knew neither who we were nor exactly why she and we were there. Even so, there was love; it showed in her face and in her voice. After we had finished eating I went to a Hammond organ down at the other end of the dining hall. My great-aunt wheeled her down to where I was, and I said, "Grandma, would you like me to play some of the old hymns?" She said, not remembering me as her great-grandson,

"Yes, young man; go right ahead." Then Grandma, in her hundred-year-old, time-worn, unisex voice started to sing along with me, "There Is a Fountain Filled with Blood." She got 99 percent of the words right except for one phrase that she invariably got wrong. Instead of "Lose all their guilty stains," she sang, "Lose all their guilty flowers." This made no sense whatsoever, but Grandma, in that cracked voice, was singing to Jesus and he heard it right.

The bass trombone position in the Boston Symphony Orchestra is held by a young Christian. Doug Yeo is his name. He believes with all of his heart that when he sits in the back row of that great orchestra playing all of that great music, he is playing to the Lord Jesus Christ. He speaks freely and publicly of making sacrifices of praise with Brahms, Beethoven, Stravinsky, and Copland. He knows that the holiness of his calling does not lie in the name of the calling but in the name of the caller.

Dr. Vida Chenoweth is a Bible translator and an ethnomusicologist. Recently she finished translating the entire New Testament into Usarufa, the language of a two-thousand-member tribe in the eastern highlands of New Guinea. She asked my wife and me to accompany her to New Guinea to assist in delivering the newly published Scriptures to the tribe. Meanwhile, as an ethnomusicologist, she has developed a system of musical analysis, derived from linguistic principles, that enables her to train students to analyze, decipher, and eventually compose in hitherto unknown and unwritten musical systems. The purpose of this is to equip Christian ethnomusicologists to encourage new Christians, especially those who still have their traditional music, to create a hymnody directly out of their own cultural resources—a welcome contrast to the importing of Western music in the name of the gospel.

Before the trek up to the Usarufa tribe, we spent some time with another tribe, the Sursurungas, on the nearby island of New Britain. This tribe, up until then, had no indigenous church music;

everything was borrowed from Western culture or from the neighboring Tolai, a larger and more prestigious tribe. Based on a quick analysis of traditional Sursurunga music, and using Scripture texts provided by the local Wycliffe translators, I composed two songs, hoping that they would come close to the indigenous style. The translators, Dr. Chenoweth, my wife, and I painstakingly memorized them. One afternoon, about a dozen Sursurungas were gathered on the veranda of the translators' house, and we began singing these two songs, not knowing what would come of it. The Sursurungas perked up and one said, "Where did you get our music?" We knew two things immediately: Dr. Chenoweth's analysis was valid, and the Sursurungas had their first indigenous church music, provided by a "redskin" (for that's what they call white people) from Illinois.

In 1969, an up-and-coming world-class jazz musician—a sax player—and his wife were nearly destroyed from heroin. His playing had gradually declined, and it was doubtful if he would ever play again. One day, in a restaurant, a "hippie" told Don Lanphere about Jesus, and he and his wife Midge turned their hearts and lives over to him. They were miraculously delivered from their habit. Musically, Don has come back. He is playing again, in jazz clubs, high schools, colleges. He does clinics; he witnesses wherever he can. He makes no bones about his love for the Lord. He has cut several records, four CD's, and is planning a fifth as of this writing. His testimony is sweet, humbled, and clear. And wherever he plays, with whomever he plays, he plays for Jesus.

Why these stories? Simply because there is something too important to overlook in relating the wide world of music making to the often narrower world of standards. We know that everyone is somehow creative and makes music and uses it in any number of ways and at any number of qualitative levels. Whether it is a 100-year-old great-grandmother forgetting the words or Doug Yeo playing in the Boston Symphony, there is something that binds them, and everybody in between, together.

Two Scripture passages, one from each testament, bear on the subject of love and unity, or what we can call brother and sister keeping. They contrast vividly. One passage (John 17:21–23) is a part of Christ's high priestly prayer: "That they may all be one; even as Thou, Father, art in Me, and I in Thee, that they also may be in Us; that the world may believe that Thou didst send Me. And the glory which Thou hast given Me I have given to them; that they may be one, just as We are one; I in Them, and Thou in Me, that they may be perfected in unity, that the world may know that Thou didst send Me. . . ."

The other passage is from a dramatically different conversation (Genesis 4:8–9): "And it came about when they were in the field, that Cain rose up against Abel his brother, and killed him. Then the Lord said to Cain, 'Where is Abel your brother?' And he said, 'I do not know. Am I my brother's keeper?'" (NASB)

First, there is Jesus' prayer, the prayer for unity. Jesus is close to the time when he will draw the whole world together at the cross. And he prays a prayer that rolls over and over itself—all about glory, love, and unity. It is not a tightly reasoned prayer but one driven by pure love and passion.

Then there is Cain's question, seemingly asked in insolence. It is a question from out of the dark of humanity's first sojourns in the vast vocabularies of sinful action.

If Christ's prayer is for unity, then it is as much a prayer about music and music making as it is about anything else. Hence, this question arises: What does it mean to be artistically unified? It does not mean doing just one kind of music and joining company with those who do the same. It means joining in with that wedding music or with someone singing out of tune and getting the words wrong or with jazz, when I like only Christian contemporary. It means being a musical part of the answer to Christ's prayer about unity.

Likewise, we can put a musical touch to Cain's question: Are we to be our brother's and sister's musical keepers? Do we have an artistic right, an aesthetic right, to ask this question in the insolence of Cain, having rid ourselves of those whose music is objectionable and who seemingly cannot be persuaded to adopt the standards we cherish? Or can we say, in the spirit of Christ, "No matter what the music is, we are always this person's keeper?" We cannot afford to respond to Christ's prayer and God's question to Cain with the indignation born of long years of exclusivism. Even though we must give God the very best, even though excellence is always worth the battle, we must strive to be at one with those who seem to get away with musical mediocrity simply by calling the Lord's blessing down upon it. We must learn to move from anger and frustration to an attitude of redemptive, nurturing, and helpful intrusion, even when we are in the presence of musical rip-off, crass commercialism, and exploitation. And in the presence of those who make music haltingly and fearfully, we must show the spirit of the one described by Isaiah as never breaking a bruised reed or extinguishing a dimly burning wick (Isaiah 42:3).

There are so many encampments in the arts, this one lashing out at the next one, and for any number of reasons. There is division over what is good and bad, moral or immoral, classical or popular, appropriate or inappropriate, old or new, familiar or strange, worshipful or not worshipful, worthy or unworthy. Whatever side of the fence somebody is on, there is always somebody over on the other side. And the tragedy of so much of this is that neither party really wants to find out about the other; the music gets in the way.

The classical musician says things like this about pop art: "It's gimmicky; it's redundant, it's clichéd; it's commercial; it's un-original; it's derivative; it manipulates; and there must be something wrong with it because it's so quickly liked." The pop musicians return the compliment: "Your music is stuck-up; it is square and behind the times; it's disorganized and too chaotic; it tries so hard to be intellectual that it has no emotional appeal; it has no meaning; it can't minister; it brings no results; it's not fun, and besides, I can't dance to it." The classicists think they are on top because they strive for greatness. The popular musicians think they have the people on their side because they are communicating—just look at the results. And so it goes, both outside and inside the body of Christ.

This is not yet the place to take sides or speak of standards, as necessary as the highest standards are. Such talk is not appropriate *until* the question of unity is addressed. We first must learn how to keep our sisters and brothers and to understand that love for them precedes the music they make, no matter how bad or good it is.

The truth of the matter is that, for the Christian, all the world is in all music making together, good and bad. Somehow, all of this music will bend its knee before God. Somehow, this great babble will turn to God's glory, from rap to Bach to the gamelan. Until we realize this, we have not earned the right to talk about standards or quality. Yet we usually begin that way, and when we compare this music with that, are we trying to think which one is better instead of discovering how they are unique and how they relate? And do we want to take the time to get to know, from the inside out, the people who make this music?

The people who have taken the time to look deeply into a huge assortment of musics, along with the people who make them, are the only ones who have earned the right to talk about standards, because they have already experienced unity and are in the process of keeping their brothers and sisters. In this sense, the entire musical world becomes one huge, mixed, and motley outcry—of joy, nearly unbearable brokenness, and fervent hope. For the Christian music maker, the task is quite simple: diversity and love and, only then, quality. This order will not dilute standards or dull critique. Instead it will position the most perceptive music making and the wisest teaching in a way that will comport with the very gospel all music making is meant to celebrate.

We began this section with some true stories. Let's end it with a parable.[1]

> In the apartment above the bakery lived Bernard, his
> mother, his baby sister, and his squalling younger brother.
> For most people in the neighborhood, Bernard being no
> exception, life was not easy and there was little time for

just sitting around. What with school, caring for his brother and sister, a part-time job bagging groceries, and peer pressure–driven basketball practice, Bernard didn't have much time for his private passion, which was learning the guitar. He had picked up an old guitar that somebody was trashing for a better one. And whenever he had a minute he would sit in the front room by the window with his boom box listening to and trying to imitate his pop heroes.

The man who owned the bakery beneath Bernard's apartment decided one day that this young prodigy needed some help, not only for Bernard's sake but to protect the neighborhood from the squeal and chaos, especially on Saturday mornings, when Bernard had more than the usual amount of time to practice. He arranged to take Bernard one night to Jesse's, a club in the neighborhood well known for its terrific live music. He even arranged for him to meet the band's guitarist, a local neighborhood hero and someone who had done just exactly what Bernard wanted to do; he had risen from obscurity to a place of modest fame and fortune. The show was over and Bernard and his guitar hero sat backstage in the dressing room. The hero listened to Bernard's licks.

"You're not half bad, kid," said the hero, "not half bad. But you've got a long way to go. You've got a lot of work to do."

Then the hero picked up his own guitar.

"This is what you'll be doing before long, maybe." The maestro let loose a string of rhythm and licks that dazzled his young listener.

"Think you could do that too?" said the hero, and handed the guitar back to Bernard and said, "Good luck. You'll need it. Keep working. Some of your stuff is okay, some isn't." And that was it.

The next Saturday no sound came from the apartment above the bakery. Bernard had tried to play, but those

words kept ringing in his ears: "Good luck. You'll need it."
He never felt emptier or further away from his music. For
a long time on Saturday mornings, no playing came from
that apartment. In fact, Bernard nearly gave up his dream
about the guitar.

That next summer, on a steamy August morning when
there was absolutely nothing to do and Bernard's friends
were too lazy even to play basketball, Bernard picked up
his guitar and, barely turning up the amplifier, started
playing. His fingers felt unaccustomed to the instrument.
But he played anyway.

There was a knock on the door. Bernard opened it. And
there stood the baker's daughter, who had just come back
to the neighborhood after being gone for a long time.

"I thought I heard some guitar playing up here," said the
baker's daughter.

"Oh yeah, it was me," said Bernard, "I just fuss around
with it."

"Well, let me hear what you are doing."

"Nah, it ain't any good."

"How do you know?"

"I just do. Someone kinda told me so."

"Well, let me listen."

It took a long time to persuade Bernard, but finally he
was willing to play a few licks, introducing them with,
"This ain't no song, it's just licks, it's just stuff I got off
tapes."

The baker's daughter said, "You know, I pluck around a
little bit, but I can't play those licks."

"You're kidding," said Bernard.

"Nope, I never learned those licks."

"Ha, ha, they're easy; they're real easy. Watch." And
Bernard, with a somewhat renewed sense of confidence,
rolled through his repertoire of licks and rhythms.

"Let me see that guitar," said the girl. She took the

instrument in her hands and made an attempt at playing one of the licks that Bernard had played.

"Is that right?" she asked.

"Ahm, not exactly," said Bernard. "It's like this." He took the guitar again and began playing. It wasn't long before the baker's daughter had learned most of the licks that Bernard had worked on.

"That's good," he said.

"Let me play you one of the things that I can play. Is that okay?"

"I guess."

She began cautiously. Right off, Bernard knew she was good, real good. But every step of the way she said, "Do you want to try that?" And Bernard, now intrigued, took the guitar in his hands and began to play the new stuff. Two hours later, the baker's daughter said, "Well, I've got to go. Can I come back next week?"

"Sure, I guess," said Bernard.

"Why don't you get some new licks for me," she said, "and I'll find some new things for you, and maybe we can both get better."

"That's cool," said Bernard.

And she went back to her work in the nearby conservatory and Bernard went back to his playing, his basketball, and his school, but especially his playing.

One summer Saturday, a few years later, Bernard, now playing regularly at Jesse's, happened down an alley. He heard a ten-year-old wailing away on a guitar. He remembered in minute detail those long-ago Saturdays, and he knew exactly what to do.

NOTES

1. Ken Medema improvised this, based on a much less interesting story that I had conjured up. With a few modifications, it is being used with his permission.

Chapter 4

THE AESTHETICS OF MUSICAL PLURALISM

There are nine and sixty ways of constructing tribal lays,
And every single one of them is right.

—RUDYARD KIPLING

If it is easy to define melody, it is much less easy to distinguish the characteristics that make a melody beautiful. The appraisal of a value is itself subject to appraisal. The only standard we possess in these matters depends on a fineness of culture that presupposes the perfection of taste. Nothing here is absolute except the relative.

—IGOR STRAVINSKY

An analogy, drawn from the Scriptures, can inform the way aesthetic standards are often applied to musical practice. The apostle Paul spent a lot of time in the epistle to the Romans talking about the law and the way it brings a knowledge of sin without providing a way out of sinfulness (chapter 7:17ff.). He tells us that we would not have come to know sin except through the law. He talks further about how we can be alive before we hear the law, but when it is revealed to us, sin becomes alive and we die.

This is exactly what can happen when we make the aesthetic cart push the practitional horse. The analogy works this way. Everybody loves music in one way or another. Everybody has a sense of quality, even though it might not always be that finely tuned. And music is everywhere. In some way everybody makes and receives music. The few who do not are to be pitied.

So here are all these music makers, enjoying what they like and liking what they enjoy. They sing, hum, whistle, croon, listen, sometimes making up a snippet or a ditty, celebrating with it, worshiping God with it, making love with it, using it to speed up milk production in cows and automobile production in assembly plants, dancing to it, and falling asleep with it.

Suddenly all of this is interrupted with the law, the aesthetic law, the laws of those with refined taste and musical etiquette, the laws of the specialist, the connoisseur, the intellectual informer. And the people who have been alive all along, making music without knowing these laws, are confronted with the lawgivers who point up their ineptitude, their omissions and commissions, and the life goes out of the riot and celebration. To paraphrase verses 10 to 13 of the same chapter, these aesthetic laws, which were designed to result in aesthetic life, turn around and take life away.

And yet, these aesthetic laws are good. The aesthetic standards themselves do not lead to our aesthetic downfall. Instead, our aesthetic weaknesses have to be revealed in order that they can be seen for what they are. But the aesthetic laws cannot be applied from the outside. Well-meaning but legalistic aesthetes cannot try to raise musical standards by applying aesthetic canons or assuming that people "ought to have enough common sense" to change once they hear the aesthetic canons. The result of this is that people may stay defeated, even though they keep trying to work things out; or they may assume that the whole exercise is silly, turn their backs on it, and go their way.

Aesthetic laws must be lived from the inside out. If, down deep, we *want* to do something with music and art besides just enjoying whatever comes along; if we really *want* to be sure that everything we take in is a work of quality, then aesthetic law can move from the outside, as something to be applied, to the inside, as something to be worked out.

In this case, there is a new teacher—*music*, in which the aesthetic laws are already at work. Aesthetic principles do not cause great music to happen, but great music keeps aesthetic principles alive. Music, coupled to the imprinted desire for excellence, then drives each one to seek out—to enable to do—the "works" of aesthetic standards.

In our spiritual lives we do not immediately attain maturity. We stumble, we fall, and we confess. We get up and continue to press on. So with music and art; there is no immediate leap into aesthetic finesse. We make music only to discover that it is not as well done as it could be; we choose a composition only to discover that there is a much better one. There is no aesthetic lapse that is too low or too grievous. Only those who do not want to change will not change. It is that simple. Great music is for everybody, not just the elitists, just as the gospel is for everybody, not just the righteous. The discernment of it comes gradually. It is learned, and everybody can learn if they want to.

But music is not our only teacher. It cannot work all of these changes by itself, although it is amazing how we can come to prefer excellence by simply living in the midst of it and drinking it in. Along with the music, we need teachers. These are not "lawgivers," but rather people who have learned to live the laws from the inside out and who know what it is to empty themselves as Christ did. They have a simple, unforced, and uncluttered love for good music, and they become one—they get down—with those whom they are wanting to help and change. They risk the accusation of being like the very ones whom they have decided to join. They mix in, they know about, they are free to converse, they may even get themselves a little bit dirty in the process. And they discover that, among all this stuff that needs aesthetic redeeming, there is also goodness, a whole lot of integrity and honesty, from which they themselves can learn.

Christ was perfection itself, becoming emptied of prerogative while visiting and becoming identified with those he came to save. But we musicians and music teachers are aesthetic "sinners" just like those whom we empty ourselves to "save." Good teachers are not pure, just a little further along. And they must never forget this.

Why Evaluate Music at All?

Why evaluate music at all? The answer is fairly straightforward. We evaluate music because human beings are incurable evaluators and music is just one of a thousand activities we evaluate. We evaluate any time there are choices. Making choices implies forming opinions; forming opinions includes evaluation. Everybody makes musical choices, sometimes through very formalized and highly theoretical mechanisms, sometimes because they are following through on what they have been taught to choose, sometimes through the workings of the "etiquettes" and social codes of their particular subculture or grouping, sometimes through simple, off-the-cuff reactions, and, in the case of many societies, through the mixture of tradition, appropriateness, and authority. In virtually all cases, choosing some music means rejecting other music. And it is fair to say that nobody, including the most enlightened and aggressive pluralists, should be expected to choose all music.

Choosing a piece of music, then, is another way of saying, "I like it." The element of musical criticism or evaluation becomes evident when somebody asks why. Even if the answer is only, "Because," some kind of valuing is implicit. Even in the briefest exchanges about why and because, something will emerge that demonstrates that the choosers have done some kind of thinking, some kind of sorting through, some kind of evaluation. Even those who choose bad music have done some kind of evaluation, not consciously to choose bad music, but to choose what seems good. The question then is not whether people evaluate music before choosing it, but how they evaluate it, by what criteria, and whether it is important to them to want to improve their evaluative capabilities.

Artistic Quality and Excellence Are Debatable

It is one thing to measure a piece of wood and another to measure a piece of music. For the one, a ruler suffices, for the other, opinion and counteropinion. The wood can be said to be exactly so long, and if used in the construction of something it will be too long, too short, or just right. This is not a matter of opinion; it is a matter of fact.

However, if we go beyond simply measuring length, thickness, and width and begin to think about the quality of the wood being used, then objective measurement stops and conjecture starts. We go from yes/no to why/why not. Is this piece more pleasing than that one? Do the grain and natural coloring of the wood contain the right contrasts or congruences? Will they occur at exactly the right "moment" in the overall effect of the furniture piece being made?

The master cabinet maker has fitted every joint with precision, matched grain and texture with care and sensitivity, and through expert planing, sanding, varnishing, and hand rubbing, has shown him- or herself to be among the finest furniture builders. The artisanship is easily measurable—the joints are perfectly closed, the measurements are true, there are no indications of cross-grain sanding, and the varnish has been rubbed out to mirrorlike opulence. But bring in the experts on design and we begin to hear opinion and counteropinion. Sides are taken. One expert may declare the piece to be totally out of sorts with the tradition while another praises it as an example of stylistic purity and elegance.

In the realm of sport, similar things happen. In the 100-meter run, the only thing that counts toward winning is the clock. Winning and losing are open-and-shut cases. The aesthetic side of running, certainly an interesting subject, simply does not enter into the final decision. The person in first place wins by so many fractions of a second, and that's that. The world's greatest runner is determined without a quibble by a timepiece.

However, in gymnastics, figure skating, or diving, the aesthetic element figures into the equation. Scores are now a mix of objectivity (Did the athlete perform all the required moves?) and subjectivity (With what kind of beauty and grace were they executed?). And all of us know how controversial some decisions can be, even turning on personal biases, political, racial, and cultural issues. These can come about only because the sport includes subjective measurement, and while aesthetics are ostensibly the only criteria, they can be adjusted by other elements with apparent impunity.

All of that to say this. Art and music can take no such refuge in objectivity. While aesthetics may be nothing more than side talk in many human activities, it is central in art and music. Music does, of course, include certain objective elements: right and wrong notes, instruments in and out of tune (although out-of-tuneness in actual performance is often a matter of debate). But the rest, comprising the majority of what music is really about, is debatable, not just at the outer extremes of great art versus terrible art, but all the time, in every quarter, from the professional critics and music makers down to the average person.

So what goes into evaluative choosing? Does evaluative choice simply boil down to a matter of taste? Do choosers always choose because they have narrowed all of their opinions and decisions down to taste alone? And, in light of musical pluralism, what is taste? Furthermore, as superficial as it may initially sound, is having good taste a biblical necessity? Where do the Scriptures talk conceptually about the components of aesthetics and taste and how to develop them?[1]

The following principle will guide us from here on: *The seeking out of quality must take place* within *musical categories, not* between *them. In the creational model of contrasting kinds, one does not judge the aesthetic quality of a cactus by talking about an orchid; in the narrower sense of species and species, pine trees and eucalyptus trees cannot be similarly compared. It makes sense, then, to apply these analogies to musical evaluation.*

This principle helps us avoid the trap of aesthetic universalism—applying a single aesthetic to multiple musical practices. We wouldn't question the beauty of the German language because it does not sound like Portuguese, without inquiring into the capabilities for beautiful expression *within* German. By the same token, we shouldn't judge the quality of a particular kind of music by comparing it to another kind. For instance, Cajun should not be considered inferior just because it does not use the same materials, structures, or idioms as progressive jazz does. This principle can also be extended into specific areas of performance styles, tone production, and instrumental timbre. We cannot, for example, criticize the practice of sliding from one pitch to another in pop and jazz just because it is undertaken in a stylistically different manner than in certain kinds of classical vocal and instrumental music. The vocal and instrumental stylings of a gifted pop or jazz musician would be out of place in a classical concert, just as those of a classical musician would in a jazz setting, unless we want to make the mistake of classicizing popular music or popularizing classical.

There is another side to the trap of aesthetic universalism. Just as a certain kind of music should not be questioned because it does not sound, say, classical, low-quality classical music should not be indiscriminately accepted because it *does* sound classical. The question of quality should not be overlooked by association: If it sounds classical, it is not necessarily good.

While our working principle helps us avoid one trap, it can set another one in return if we are not careful. This one lies in the carelessness with which we might justify the growing proliferation of musical styles, substyles, and sub-substyles, and an equal number of labels used to identify and artificially separate them. For instance, in the field of rock, should there be separate criteria for evaluating classic rock, heavy metal, acid, house, hip hop, punk, jazz rock, country rock, thrash, and soft rock? To some people, these are different languages, and if different languages, then different criteria must be applied.

If we can agree that there is no universal aesthetic covering all musics, we should also agree that there is not an infinity of aesthetics or aesthetic subtypes, separately designed for each new twist or paraphrase. The final absurdity of this would be the creation of a maze of discreet, personalized, self-constructed aesthetics, each one intended to justify each thing done: This is mine; it is unique; it is different; it is separate; therefore it is good. This may be nothing other than intellectual or subcultural narcissism disguised as aesthetics. Yet in many ways our culture, in a strange combination of privatism and relativism, has come to this place. Each activity, no matter how similar it might be to another, is considered by its practitioners to be unique, free of value judgment from another quarter. Each is self-justified, therefore above question. These particles of pseudouniqueness are the opposite of what true pluralism is intended to be: a relational, nurturing intercourse of things, in which communities learn from each other, values are shared, excellence expected, and standards maintained.

The Distinction Between Musical Languages, Dialects, and Styles

In order to avoid the pitfalls of narrow exclusivism and sloppy inclusivism and to build toward a workable aesthetic of pluralism, we need to distinguish among musical languages, dialects, and styles. An analogy from literature, followed by a brief discussion of a few concepts, should get us started.

The beginning of Gerard Manley Hopkins's poem "The Windhover"[2] goes this way:

> I caught this morning morning's minion, king-
> dom of daylight's dauphin,
> Dapple-dawn-drawn Falcon, in his riding
> Of the rolling level underneath him steady air, and striding
> High there, how he rung upon rein of a wimpling wing
> In his Ecstasy! then off, off forth on a swing. . . .

Someone else might describe the scene this way:

This morning, early on, I saw a quite beautiful bird. It glided and hung steady almost as if the air were solid, as if there were no gravity and he could not fall.
The bird was, I believe, a falcon, or kestrel, those coloring was further intensified by the dawn's light. There was no doubting the beauty of this graceful creature—a favorite of the morning itself.

Another puts it this way:

At approximately 5:13 of the morning in question, a lone member of the species *falco tinnunculus*, also known as the kestrel, appeared

over the horizon, twelve o'clock high. Air currents, coupled to the
bird's unusual ability to hover, were such that the usual glide pattern
was unusually extended and effortless. While, from the position the
observer was in, accurate color markings could not be exactly
determined, it was obvious that, through a combination of the angled
sunlight and the bird's plumage, a mottled effect was evident. Some
might call this attractive.

Yet another:

I can't find words, yet God helping I will. I had to get up early—you
know I've taken on extra work to get the kids through school—and on
my way—I was walking because Jim took the car in for a valve job—I
saw something that, well, made me feel like heaven and earth had
been made into one little special eternity—just for me—I hope that
doesn't sound too me-ish; my therapist's been helping me with that.
Where was I? Right. I saw this scrumptious little bird, colored like
those new stretch pants on sale at K Mart and I got all goose
bumpy. . . .

One more:

> As I got up one early morn,
> Before the sun the day had borne,
> I saw a bird whose vibrant hue
> Would thrill the heart of me and you.
>
> She swooped and climbed on feathered wing;
> And sometimes hung, as on a string.
> She owned the dawn and I must say,
> "I pray I'll spy her one more day."
>
> Some call her kestrel, others, friend.
> For me, my wonder has no end:
> Poems are made with foolish word,
> But only God can make a bird. Thank you.

And:

I saw the daggondest thing long about sunup. Some city folk with
binoculars, bird books, and wicker baskets call 'em kestrels. Down
thisaway we call 'em danglers 'cause of the funny way they float b'fore

takin' off like a greased goose. They sure a damsight purtier
than crows. Fact, I'd like ta lay holt of a buncha their feathers for the
wife's hat. Dang, I don't know which was purtier, the sun acomin' up
or that little bird. All's I got to say is they belonged t'onenuther.

Finally:

Like real early I saw this awesome bird? I'm like wow because
he flew maaan like he was on some kind of trip I mean where did he
pick up on that groove? I go I can't believe this; it was like sometimes
he was like hung from some awesome hook and then he goes
totally fast. His colors were like some kind of far-out light show?
It was cool man, real cool.

Nobody should call these different languages, just to ensure
that they are on equal aesthetic footing. Different ways of speaking
English, they are; but different languages, no. They encompass a
variety of styles; all are in some way expressive, each making an
attempt to paint some kind of picture. Anybody except the most
sealed-off provincial can make sense of each and relate each one to
the rest. And it is possible for nearly anybody with a reasonably
informed aesthetic sense to comment in some way on their quality,
despite regional, procedural, dialectical, and stylistic differences.

The point of all of this is that we cannot hide behind careless
statements about differences in languages in order to imply the
existence of separate standards for evaluation. We must face up to
more precise difference among dialects, styles, vernaculars, polish,
coarseness, efficiency, inefficiency, and ultimately quality. All of
the examples, while coming from different subcultural quarters, can
be submitted to certain general evaluative criteria.

With the foregoing analogy as a start, we can now ask two primary questions. The first is: What is a musical language and how
does it differ from musical dialects and perhaps musical styles? This
is a music theory question, but you need not be alarmed. We will
not be using any musical terms or concepts that you do not already
know about. The second question is: Once we clarify the language/
dialect/style question, how can we go about evaluating all these
differing and related musics?

In order to answer the first question, let's use spoken language again as an example and then we'll switch over to music. All languages have an alphabet (or some other basic sound or sign system), a vocabulary, and a way of knitting discrete pieces of the vocabulary together into structures that communicate meaning. Languages may appear in groups that, while not commonly sharing everything, share enough to be considered related. What they do share and don't share determine the extent to which they can be mutually understood. Vocabulary is often the key. If different languages share much of the same vocabulary, then it makes less of a difference if the grammars or even pronunciations differ. For example, even though the grammatical constructions in German vary significantly from those of English, I can make pretty decent sense out of a German sentence if I have a working knowledge of German vocabulary. I can simply rearrange the words according to the grammatical rules for my own language. This will not only give me a good feeling for what the German sentence is saying, but I'll slowly begin to get an inkling of how German grammar works, if I keep at it. Admittedly, this works best when I'm listening to or reading German, not trying to speak it. But since we're talking primarily about listening, the analogy remains useful.

But this associational process will not work in languages that share nothing in common. If I speak Hungarian and hear or see Chinese, nothing connects. I am literally facing completely different languages whose alphabetic, vocabularial, and syntactical processes go in entirely different directions. Thus Hungarian and Chinese, or Chinese and Sanskrit, are by strictest definition separate languages.

So here is a principle: *Two languages can be called separate languages if there is no alphabetic and vocabularial connection between them. There might be structural similarities, but they are of no help without alphabetic and vocabularial connections.*

Musical languages are uniquely separate when their basic pitch systems, melodic and possible harmonic vocabularies, and structural devices cannot interface with those of another musical system without major compromise or forced adjustment. Dialects are variants on languages, and styles are variants on dialects. Stating matters this way implies that, contrary to the number of discrete spoken languages, there might be fewer completely separate musical languages in the world than there are related musical languages, dialects, and styles. The responsibility for sorting these out rests with music theorists and ethnomusicologists, particularly those who have gone beyond the cultural and anthropological aspects of world music into the deeper questions of musical syntax and structure. We can call these scholars the linguists of music.[3]

From the foregoing, we can divide world musics into three basic groups:

a. Musical languages that are separated from each other, with no apparent systemic links. An example would be Tibetan chant and reggae.

b. Musical systems that are related at a deep systemic level but separated as to vocabulary and idiom. An example of this would be twelve-bar blues and Lutheran chorales. A more sophisticated example would be the music of George Gershwin and that of J. S. Bach.

c. Musics that, in addition to being related at a deeper level, are styles of each other. Examples of this would be progressive jazz and bebop, or punk rock and acid rock.

Fortunately, we can enjoy many kinds of music without having to have extensive theoretical knowledge of how they work. Yet this nagging question comes up when we hear a piece of music that doesn't quite fit our listening vocabulary. Experientially it might sound unrelated, as if it were a separate language, even though the music theorists might insist that it is one of a group of closely related dialects.

This is where we have to recognize that what our cultural ears tell us may be quite different than what our intellectual or theoretical systems do. That is, taking *in* music—the affective/experiential side of music making—can be quite different than thinking *about* music. Musical sounds are not the same as musical treatises. A music theorist can take bebop, Cajun, Mozart, and Prokofiev and show how they flow out of a fundamentally similar way of using pitches taken from a common inventory, knit together in commonly related ways, and using similar formal structures. Music theorists are trained to listen, perceive, and report in ways that untrained listeners aren't. Yet neither the trained nor the untrained can be expected to build enthusiastic and discerning listening skills on theory alone. The intellectual connections in no way guarantee an experiential connection.

Something else has to take place to displace the cognitive vacuum and the perceptual distance, namely repeated and open-minded listening. This process is not unlike the way children learn to speak several languages at once. They do not study language theory, grammar, or structure in order to accomplish this. Nor do they hear anything about the aesthetic values of human speech. They simply hear the languages and jump in midstream. By virtue of a desire to communicate; through repetition, trial, and error, *coupled to the styles and qualities of expression of those with whom they speak*, they learn languages, dialects, styles, and idiomatic nuances. Later on, in formal studies of grammar and syntax, they learn to think *about* what they have long ago learned to think *in*.

Meanwhile, something can happen with musical perception that cannot happen with spoken languages. Since music does not have the same kind of propositional specificity that spoken language does, sometimes we find that we can jump—even leapfrog over— theoretically separate musical languages, creating sonic, textural, rhythmic, and other linkages without knowing or caring that, at base, the two musics may be as systemically disjunct as Chinese and Spanish are. For example, someone who is deeply attached to nineteenth-century Italian opera may, without any effort, be able perceptually to identify with Tibetan chant. The leap is experiential and affective rather than systemic or theoretical. Consequently, we are faced with two affective/experiential possibilities in music, both of which can be overcome or experienced without theoretical help: (1) we can experience great perceptual distance between two very closely related systems; (2) we can experience perceptual nearness even though two musical systems might be at a great distance theoretically. In both cases, the key ingredient is open-mindedness and repeated listening.

Now let's bring the language/dialect/style model closer to home and connect it to the many musical practices in America. Admittedly, we will be making rather broad strokes. But if we choose the right ones, we can fill out any number of details without contradicting the basic outline. The Western musical tradition—classical, popular, and ethnic—comprises *one basic musical language system* that all Euro-Americans know and use to create and interrelate virtually all dialects and styles. There are all kinds of classical, popular, and ethnic musical dialects and styles: German, Italian, English, Swedish, Dutch, and so on. And there are also distinctly American dialects, ways of putting sounds together that seem to speak with a character of their own, even though they may reach back into earlier music or around into other contemporary styles and dialects. These dialects can be sensed in the music of Aaron Copland, Stephen Foster, George Gershwin, John Philip Sousa, Hoagy Carmichael, Leonard Bernstein, and Merle Haggard. They can be picked up in hymn tunes like "Amazing Grace," "What Can Wash Away My Sins?", and the hauntingly beautiful music of the Civil War, especially that of the Confederacy. Appalachian folk and hymn tunes ("I Wonder as I Wander," "What Wondrous Love Is This"), while bearing an earlier imprint of the folk musics of England, Scotland, and Ireland, still have a peculiarly American "accent."

But what about jazz? Why did we not include it above? By all accounts, it is America's music, America's musical gift to the rest of the world. Here's the reason. Jazz is a prime example of an interrelation or fusion of distinct languages. The musical languages and dialects of Africa encountered and merged with the language of Western music through the obscenity of slavery. Through a profound synthesis and evolution, the world now has a rich cross-dialect—there is no other word for it—with innumerable styles and practices: blues, jazz, bebop, swing, progressive jazz, rhythm and blues, rock 'n' roll, rock, and so on. There is no way they can be successfully separated. They have influenced music worldwide. We can't listen to gospel, Cajun, Christian contemporary, rock, country, or twentieth-century classical without recognizing their influences.

We can only conclude that, in the broadest sense, America uniquely owns a variety of separate but interrelated dialects: Euro-American and African American. The beauty of this phenomenon is that all of the distinct musics that we possess have survived and overcome the older (and we hope outdated) notion of America as a melting pot.

Aesthetic Principles Derived from the Foregoing

In light of musical diversity and the inborn love that all of us have for music, coupled to the possible difference between loving music and properly evaluating it, what should happen as we continue to diversify musically? How do we know what's good? Should we bother to find out? Even though we cannot claim to find a universal aesthetic, how do we keep ourselves from aesthetic anarchy? The following principles seek to put all of this together in as simple a way as possible.

1. *Our personal capability for evaluating a piece of music will be in direct proportion to our perceptual distance from it. The nearer we are* practitionally and perceptually *to a musical system, knowing it from the inside, the more capable we are of making musical judgments on our own. The further away it is, the less capable we will be to evaluate it.* This means that when we stand "outside" a musical system we must depend on those who are "insiders"—the indigenous practitioners of the language, dialect, or style—to show us if and how they evaluate what they do. We must say "if" because some societies may not talk "aesthetically" about musical values (though this does not mean that they do not make musical choices). Further, some societies may not possess a body of music that

includes both good and bad. Somehow the "bad" disappears and only the "good" remains, comprising the entirety.

2. *The nearer musical dialects or styles are to each other, the more they may be subject to common evaluation.* This is most apparent in groups of languages found in the same civilizational gathering that is part of a classical culture. Using language as an example, Italian, French, Portuguese, Spanish, English, German, and others, while superficially different languages, have literatures that are judged by fairly common aesthetic principles. The same is true of Western art music, irrespective of any national, regional, idiomatic, or chronological differences that might exist among them. Thus the music, say, of Palestrina (sixteenth-century Italian), Elgar (nineteenth-century English), Fauré (nineteenth-century French), Brahms (nineteenth-century German), Ives (early twentieth-century American), Badings (twentieth-century Dutch), and Stravinsky (twentieth-century Russo-American) are all subject to a classical Western aesthetic.

3. *At the popular and folk levels, any number of musics may be falsely perceived by insiders to be separate languages, when in a theoretical sense they are only separate dialects or styles of the same language. This is where the insider/outsider paradigm undergoes the most tension and generates the most debate.* There are two different elements at work here. The first derives out of the way music quickly absorbs the environments in which it is repeatedly made. (This was discussed at some length in chapter 2.) Musical style and social internalization, ethnic pride, dignity, and independence merge so effectively that the music appears to be uniquely equivalent to the entire culture. Consequently, it is difficult for the insiders to perceive the music as anything other than a separate language. This will be all the more true if the music is directly linked to the culture's religious and ethical systems. Then musical practice is not only equivalent to the culture, but believed to take on the qualities of the religious system itself.

So while music theorists talk objectively about dialectical and stylistic similarities among different cultural groupings, the members of the groups in question may assume the musics to be fundamentally separated. The insiders' perceptions of quality should be carefully heard, but it will probably turn out that a collection of any number of folk and ethnic "aesthetics" can be synthesized into a common aesthetic. *This will be true to the extent that the different enclaves are the ethnically popular counterparts of a common classical culture.*

In certain segments of contemporary American popular culture a different kind of enclaving, more akin to group narcissism—a corporate me-ness—resulting in strong musical provincialism may occur. Types of music are narrowed down by their exclusive connection to particular functions, and substyles of substyles are considered to be separate practitional and perceptual domains, separate "languages." This is the musical equivalent of: "This is me; this is my style; my style is my language; it is my pleasure; this is my world; I say what goes; my definition of quality (if I feel one to be relevant at all) is mine alone; yours does not pertain and mine is sufficient." In the field of linguistics, an idiolect is a "language" that only the speaker understands. Music making in the context of group narcissism may be a socialized version of this.

Aesthetic evaluation, in these cases, must come mainly from the outside, because the insiders are so taken up with what serves and pleases them that it does not—need not—occur to them that there are evaluative relationships between what they do and what any other subgroup does. Nor is it relevant that larger questions of discernment be asked or answered. Thus those who offer any kind of aesthetic critique are perceived to be absolutists, squares, or meddlers.

Assuming we have established some way of steering between the extremes of aesthetic universalism and undifferentiated relativism, and assuming that there is a way to go about seeking and finding quality while enjoying musical pluralism, we need to ask one more question. It's a pesky one, because at first glance it appears to reconfirm the issue of aesthetic universalism.

Pluralism and Musical Values: Can One Music Be Better than Another?

Can one music be better than another? We hinted at the answer to this question in chapter 1. Now we need to take it up more fully to see if scriptural principles open the way for a concept of musical values that keeps us from falling back into the traps of aesthetic universalism and valueless relativity. Once again, we find the answer in biblical comments about God's handiwork. Here is a principle. *Regarding the creation, the Scriptures make simultaneous provision for the intrinsic goodness of all things and one thing being better than another.* Here's the same principle stated in a shortened and slightly awkward form: In the creation, there is a difference between intrinsic goodness and better-than-ness.

First of all, the creation is filled with all manner of creatures. Each was declared to be good—to possess intrinsic, not borrowed, worth. This intrinsic worth takes precedence over function, usefulness, size, shape, quantity, and extent. Thus each creature, each kind, each species, is equally good. The Scriptures declare this unequivocally.

However, in the face of declared intrinsic worth, the Scriptures do allow for qualitative hierarchies in the creation. Parts of it are clearly said to be better or more desirable than others. On the one hand, there is talk of deserts, wastelands, thorns, thistles, moles and bats, unseemly parts, clean and unclean, and so on. In contrast, there are springs of water, cedars, spices, oases, the sun in all its glory, gold, milk, sapphires, and honey. By the way they are spoken of, there is no doubt that they are considered "better-than." This allowance for better-than-ness is probably best represented in the description of the New Jerusalem (Revelation 21:10ff.), where the most desirable and beautiful parts of the present creation are used as metaphors for that which, because of its absolute newness and differentness, cannot be described any other way.

So we have it. God makes things; God makes them well; God calls them good; and God has no trouble saying that one thing may be better than another. If this does not trouble God whose handiwork far outstrips ours, why should it trouble us? *Consequently, there should be nothing wrong with the discovery and disclosure of the coexistence of goodness and better-than-ness in musical and artistic practice.* This approach flies in the face of the kind of loose, generalized rhetoric in the area of multicultural studies that rejects almost any discussion of relative goodness. It calls for a more discerning kind of thinking, especially on the part of Christians. It condemns exclusivism while allowing for hierarchies of values. And just as the Scripture never calls for doing away with a dandelion because it isn't an orchid, there should be no call for doing away with a musical type even though it, in the larger sense, might not be as-good-as.

The scriptural soundness of this approach brings a dimension to pluralism that corrects two common errors in cross-cultural or cross-typological thinking: (1) sameness and equal rights are not the same thing; (2) intrinsic goodness does not cancel out the concept of better-than-ness. Looking intelligently into the paradoxical coexistence of these two realities calls for a combination of wisdom, global openness, and care. The inquiry simply cannot be avoided.

So even though there may be qualitative hierarchies, pluralism remains organic, as much in world music as in the creation as in the body of Christ. All the parts are both important and in need of each other even though some might be better than others. Intrinsic worth binds all together, even when something may be said to be better than something else.

One more wrinkle must be ironed out before we're finished. Things in the creation that might be less desirable in one context become highly desirable, or better-than, in another. *In other words, better-than-ness may not be hierarchical but functional.* For example, the apostle Paul speaks pejoratively of wood, hay, and straw as compared to gold, silver, and precious stones, in the context of God's fiery testing of our works (1 Corinthians 3:12–15). Because the wood, hay, and straw represent questionable steward-ship, they will be consumed while the gold, silver, and precious stones will outlast the flame. But in shipbuilding, wood is the preferred material. Animals cannot survive by eating gold and jewels; they need hay and straw. And to fill a manger with precious stones simply because they may have more hierarchical value would starve a herd of cattle.

Bringing all this around to the subject of musical pluralism, we can understand that even though music x, in the abstract, might be argued to be better than music y, it might not be appropriate for a certain context, while the other would be highly desirable. In other words, musical value is strongly context dependent. To conjecture that Bach is better than bluegrass is one thing, but to perform one of his fugues in the middle of a hoedown is another. Unless we are willing to say that the entire cultural and ethnic context, which includes the hoedown, is aesthetically suspect, we cannot question the worth and value of bluegrass as the best kind of music for that context. The real task is to find the best bluegrass while weeding out the worst.

NOTES

1. Whenever the Scriptures mention anything approximating what we call art—making buildings, music, dancing, designing, or weaving—words like *skill, craftsmanship, understanding, wisdom,* or *wholeheartedness* are used. Two key passages are Exodus 31:1ff.; 35:10–35; and 36:1ff.
2. Norman H. Mackenzie, ed., *The Poetical Works of Gerard Manley Hopkins* (Oxford: Clarendon Press, 1990), p. 144.
3. For example, two contrasting strands of linguistic thought, tagmemics and transformational-generational linguistics, have each contributed to the field of music theory: Vida Chenoweth, *Melodic Perception and Analysis* (Ukurumpa, E. H. D., Papua New Guinea: Summer Institute of Linguistics, 1972); Fred Lehrdal and Ray Jackendoff, *A Generative Theory of Tonal Music* (Cambridge: MIT Press, 1983).

Chapter 5

PERSONAL EXCELLENCE, SUCCESS, AND COMPETITION

> "And let every skillful man among you come, and make all that the Lord has commanded. . . ." And all the skillful men who were performing all the work of the sanctuary came, each from the work he was performing, and they said to Moses, "The people are bringing much more than enough for the construction work which the Lord commanded us to perform."
>
> —EXODUS 35:10; 36:4–5 (NASB)

A long time ago, before the business world took it and equated it with financial success and corporate one-upmanship; centuries before the world of sport laid hold of it and made it equal to winning at all costs; before higher education appropriated it, filled promotional material with it, manipulated students, parents, alumni, and donors, and more than occasionally lied about it; before aesthetic prescriptionists snatched it up and turned it into perfectionism and exclusivism; and centuries before many Christians borrowed it to describe and validate just about anything that brings results; this great word *excellence* appeared in Scripture, in simple, plainspoken, yet radical settings.[1]

"Finally, brothers, whatever is true, whatever is noble, whatever is right, whatever is pure, whatever is lovely, whatever is admirable—if anything is excellent or praiseworthy—think about such things" (Philippians 4:8, NIV).

A simple reordering of certain words will help make a point: "Finally, brethren, whatever is *true*, whatever is *right*, whatever is *pure*; whatever is *noble*, whatever is *lovely*, whatever is *admirable*—if anything is excellent or praiseworthy—think about such things."

The key words have been placed in this order: true, right, pure; noble, lovely, admirable. This allows the concept of excellence to be viewed two ways. First, excellence is the *what* of living: truth, rightness, and purity. Second, excellence is the *quality*, the style, the tone, of life: nobility, loveliness, and admirableness. It can be put this way. We are to spend our lives being true, pure, and in the right. But we are to go about this nobly, with loveliness, and in an admirable and exemplary way. Thus truthfulness, rightness, and purity of heart are coupled to a quality of soul. Uprightness is coupled to elegance; the truth is done beautifully. We are to proceed from loving the truth to living the truth elegantly and admirably; in short, we are to become living epistles.

There is another place in Scripture where excellence is used in a way similar to that of the Philippians passage. First Corinthians 12:31b speaks of a way of excellence that goes far beyond some of the key gifts necessary to the life of the church: wisdom, knowledge, faith, healing, miracles, prophecy, distinguishing of spirits, tongues, and interpretations of tongues. These gifts, as important to each other as the hand is to the eye or the head to the feet (verse 21), are valueless without the more excellent way of love (lovingness, loving-kindness, loveliness), spoken of in the entirety of chapter 13.

Now let's try for a definition of excellence—the simpler the better—that is faithful to these Scriptures. *Excellence is the process*—note that word *process—of becoming better than I once was*. I am not to become better than someone else is or even like someone else. Excelling is simply—and radically—the process of improving over yesterday or, in the apostle Paul's words, "pressing on" (Philippians 3:14, NIV). Whatever the standards or conditions are, I am to strive to better them and to seek higher ones. In fact, I might even be able to raise ones that exist.

Thus excellence is both absolute and relative. It is absolute because we are commanded to pursue it. There is simply no option. Whatever is excellent, think on it so as to do something about it. In 1 Corinthians 14:12 Paul couples thinking about to doing when he speaks of excelling with gifts that build up the church. And in

Proverbs 21:29 we are told that an upright man gives thought to his ways. Whatever our ways are—our doing—they must be driven by excelling thought.

In this absolute sense, excellence is directly connected to stewardship. Perhaps it can be better stated this way: Since we are to be good stewards and since we are commanded to press on and become better than we once were, *excellence is the norm of stewardship*. There are no exceptions. It is commanded of everyone. Excelling is to be normal. It is not reserved for the elite, the bright, the culturally advanced, the rich, the powerful, the beautiful people, or those with biological, intellectual, musical, or socioeconomic head starts. Nor does the pursuit of excellence necessarily signify how any of these people got this way.

Excellence is relative because it is set in the context of growth, of growing up into, of striving, wrestling, hungering, thirsting, pressing on from point to point and achievement to achievement. Excellence is not steady state. It is sojourn and progress, reformation and change. We are unequally gifted—no two people are alike—hence no two people can equally achieve. But the real point, the scriptural point, is that whatever we are, whoever we are, we can all be better than we once were. Name the activity, name the gift, name the call, and the commandment to excel in excelling stares at all of us, all of the world, square in the face. The question of God to every Christian is simply this: "Having achieved thus and so, what is your next move?"

Consequently, the bedrock of excellence does not consist simply in these popularized criteria: being number one, being in the top 10 percent, winning first place, accolades, prizes, awards, the select few being the excellent. Rather, it lies in the exercise of far different but wonderful and extraordinary things: truth, purity, rightness, loveliness, honor, and admirableness.

Now that we have an idea of what excellence is, we need to say what is it not.

1. *Excellence is not perfection.* Quite simply, we have no observable working model to show us what perfection is. If we pursue it anyway, and most of us do, we are pursuing an

abstraction, and a neurosis-producing one at that. We know how frantic, paranoid, defeated, afraid, and even despairing we can become if we let this thing called perfectionism overtake us. And those times we think we have found it—I got 100 percent in this, or a ten in that, or I just played it through perfectly right before my lesson and I can't understand why I blew it—at these rare times, we know way down inside that these were not perfection but just transient, limited, and superficial correctness. And they are always objectively measurable. In baseball parlance, a perfect game only means no hits or walks; it does not mean that the pitcher pitched perfectly; even less does it mean that the pitcher is perfect or that this feat will ever be repeated again. If everybody batted 1.000, professional baseball would still be in the top half of the first inning and would stay that way forever, unless all pitchers pitched perfect games, in which case there would be one eternal baseball game, continuing in a scoreless tie. The very quality that makes a complete baseball game or season possible, namely, imperfection, is the very same quality that, in this and other circumstances, we try to avoid all the time.

In music, even if nobody ever played any wrong notes, that would only be the beginning. What is perfect tempo, perfect phrasing, perfect interpretation, a perfect sense of style? For that matter, is the composition that I want to perfectly perform perfect to begin with? If so, how do we prove it? If not, what do we do about all the imperfect music that so many of us love with such passion? Is our passion therefore imperfect? And so on.

What we do know about perfection is that both times it appeared on earth, it was refused: the first time by two perfect beings who turned their backs on it; the second time, by all of us, inherently imperfect, who hated the holy and perfect one to the point of crucifying him. But this state of imperfection, in which we are all somehow caught, does not keep us from the pursuit of excellence— becoming better than we once were. In fact, this very pursuit, this gracious provision of a loving God who cannot personally know what it means to improve over Himself, rescues us from the terrifying thought of never being perfect here on this earth. We can all take comfort in this simple fact: While we move from good to better to best; while we endeavor to become better than we were; while we excel, Christ perfects our excelling and presents it to the Father. This is grace, this is atonement, this is powerful, this is wonderfully comforting, and this is the way it is.

2. *Excellence is not being better than somebody else, nor is it even being like him, her, or them.* Considering the very simple fact that God created each of us as individuals and is quite content with His handiwork in each of us, which is better: besting someone else or trading my created individuality for theirs? In either case, I risk surrendering my uniqueness and I essentially imply that God should have had second thoughts while putting me together in my mother's womb.

We cannot become better than we once were with other people's gifts. Furthermore, we have no way of knowing how genuine or excelling they are at the time we are trying to emulate them. After all, they might, at that very moment, be trying to be like us in order to be better than somebody else, and we end up chasing each other in some kind of stewardly catch-22. And when we confuse steady and stewardly work with workaholism, we end in a dilemma that has put a stranglehold on far too many sincere young Christians, all in the name of some vague idea of Christian perfection.

3. *Excellence is not winning, although it may include it.* Even when we do win, this is not the same as beating someone else. Rather, it is nothing other than the act of becoming better than I once was in the presence of those who, for a time, may not be as far along on the statistical side of the game as I might be. But we must bear in mind: The person who comes in second or tenth may have come further along in the *real* art of excelling, further along than the person who came in first. Unfortunately, the world and its measuring systems have no way of taking this into account.

But God does. The one who made more average people than any other kind knows the interior glory of a C student excelling by continuing to earn C's. God also knows that we have masked elitism by calling it excellence. We have to remember that God loves and honors people who are working at the edge of their stewardship, win or lose, gifted or normal. God knows, and we should too, that for some the pursuit of excellence might mean backing off of earning A's and going to B's or staying put in the corporate world instead of moving up the ladder. Far too many people have striven for excellence falsely at tremendous expense to their spiritual, physical, emotional, and social lives. This is nothing other than selling one's soul to the company store—it's really a mixture of intemperance and idolatry—and unless we guard against it all the time, it will dog us, whatever our calling is, for the rest of our lives.

4. *Excellence is not on-again-off-againism.* It is not snatching up a fragment of quality here and a snippet of improvement there and using them as a facade, an overlay, or a veneer. It is not accretion or tokenism. It is not adding Pachelbel's "Canon" or Handel's *Messiah* or Take Six or John Updike or "Georgia on My Mind" to a basic diet of soaps, schlock, and kitsch. Excellence is organic, integrative, and totally reforming. It is a quality of life, not a quality occasionally added to it. Excellence is thus directly linked to sojourn, and sojourn is not going in circles, nor is it haphazard wandering. It is purposeful doing, even though the doing might be so new and so risky that it might appear for a while that we are moving in the dark.

This is where the story of Abraham is so important. God called him to leave very affluent, power-laden, and pleasant surroundings and to make his way to a land that God would later show him (Genesis 12:1). Abraham did just this, believing God all along, trusting God all the while, moving from circumstance to circumstance and crisis to crisis. Sometimes he acted wisely, other times foolishly, but always in good faith, always with a single heart, and always pressing on. This moving in the dark and trusting God is not equivalent to sloppy planning and then calling on God for a quick antidote, nor is it moving in the dark for its own sake. It is part of the life of trust and, in so many human circumstances, part of the heavy price of creativity.

5. *Excellence is not assuming that my way of doing things is automatically excellent simply because I intellectually agree that I need excellence.* To have ideas is one thing; to live out ideas—be living epistles—is quite another. Becoming better than I once was assumes action upon an idea—going from concept to conviction to action.

6. *Excellence is not just practicality and favorable results.* Just because something sells or ministers or persuades or changes things does not mean that excellence has taken place. Commerce, the media, and even a good part of the church have come to define excellence this way: If it works, it must be excellent; if this technique persuades, if that protocol saves a soul, if this piece of music leads to worship, if that approach collects enough votes to elect, we have achieved excellence. Nonsense.

One of the most insidious manifestations of pseudoexcellence today is the substitution of production for content. Through any number of technological enhancements, manipulations, substitutions, and replications, the less-than-excelling are made bigger than life, from advertising to political campaigning to the recording studio. And what about the Christian world? How many times have we lip-synched Jesus? How many applause tracks accompany the average Christian television program? How many musicians use taped accompaniments to enhance content, to import authenticity, and give the lie to what a local congregation should be authentically doing even if it cannot do it quite as well as the one down the street?

Perhaps we have it all backwards or upside down. Instead of little people trying to become someone they are not—trying to overpower with technique—God might just be wanting all the little people, *created that way in the first place*, to stay their own size so that divine power can come down on them and break down strongholds the divine way, with the straightforward foolishness of the gospel.

In the face of all of this glut of power, size, and glory, what is excellence anyway? The answer is brief.

Excellence is authenticity. Excellence is temperance in all things. It is servanthood. It is loving-kindness. It is sojourn. It is esteeming another better than oneself. It is meekness, brokenness, personal holiness, greatness of soul. It is peaceableness, gentleness, perseverance, hunger and thirst. Wherever we are in the quest of these, there is more. Excellence is for everybody. It is commanded and we must pursue it. There are no exceptions and no stopping in the pursuit of it. It is a process, not an event. And, in the final analysis, there are no earthly measurements for it. The pursuit of it is entirely personal and the final judge as to its validity will be a God whose wise creatorhood, sustenance, and expectations are worth far more than blue ribbons, accolades, recording contracts, or Grammys.

Success and Competition

In the biblical sense, succeeding is the unavoidable symptom of stewardship, improving where improvement is valid and achieving where achievement is valid. Therefore, we can say that succeeding and excelling are twin words, each describing a simple personal concept: improving over what I once was or finding, in the apostle Paul's words, a more excellent way and pursuing it mightily.

As with excellence, success is not an event but a process, a lifelong one, comprising balance, integration, peace, rest, and temperance. All of these are pulled into accord with each other by the working of a faithful conscience. Competition is the act of striving *against* any kind of atrophy, retrogression, inversion, or stasis, each of which may be masking as, or competing against, excelling or succeeding. It is also the act of striving *with* others who likewise are striving well.

Competition, like excellence and success, is also a process. It may take place publicly, privately, or corporately; in sport, art, work, worship, marriage, or hobby. In these contexts, a person competes *with*, not against; not to beat, but to stretch, someone. What we usually call winning is simply a structural and cultural artifice that can be measurably attached to competition. But, to the extent that artifice and culture might combine to make winning the "only thing," this kind of winning is morally bankrupt and, in the eternal sense, completely irrelevant. One can compete and, by these exterior artifices, lose, yet personally excel and succeed. For a Christian, winning is to be seen more as a symptom of having striven than a cause for striving. Competition and winning are, by consequence, just as much a matter of temperance as succeeding is. To go all out is to strive mightily, but only in terms of one's conscience and capabilities, not at the expense of health, faith, friends, family, or ethics. In an even larger sense, competition is not just for the healthy, rich, famous, and gifted. It is for alcoholics, gluttons, addicts, abusers, perfectionists, daily sinners, and sojourners, each in a profound way having to strive mightily and, frequently losing, still striving to win. And in God's eyes, these competitions and strivings make those in big-time sport, art, and business pale by comparison.

The Scripture uses strong, everyday, often coarse language to press the messages about excelling, competing, and succeeding, whether by metaphor or anecdote. No one can avoid these predominating verbs, scattered throughout both testaments: running, warring, wrestling, striving, walking, fighting, panting after, going up against, and so on. They are there to show the gritty reality of the struggle each of us faces daily.

As to music making, the implications of the foregoing are straightforward. The music world, perhaps more than ever before, has made competition, succeeding, and excelling into idols. In many quarters, artistic competition is ruthless, greed is rampant, and excelling is in direct proportion to commercial success. The force and attraction of notoriety and stardom have turned countless young people into puppets, manipulatable and morally forgetful. It has become very difficult for anyone who truly loves the many musics of today to know where to draw the line. Christian music is no guarantee of safe refuge; the same sins that dog the world dog the church. Record sales, Grammys, Doves, ASCAP and BMI incentives, royalties, and the like have become nearly inseparable from ministry, worship, and personal devotion. For the average young musician, it is difficult to think of succeeding and excelling back home, all alone and unknown, at the synthesizer, cloistered in a practice room, while trying to take the next lonely, unnoticed step toward some ideal set up by a distant superstar or a demanding teacher. Ministry and fame have become so equated with each other that it is nearly impossible to think of anything but fame if one contemplates a ministry in music.

But for the dedicated Christian, music making has to begin and continue in the same way all other activities do. Personal excelling, competing, and succeeding are intensely personal and, in the most fundamental sense, disconnected from what has happened to someone else or what the culture's definitions, standards, behaviors, and expectations might be.

NOTES

1. One of the main tenets of this book is that people are more important than their handiwork, just as God is more important than the creation. Even though this brief chapter is more of a general nature, it is being included for its application to everyday excellence for everybody, which, of course, includes music making.

Chapter 6

GENERAL ISSUES IN MUSICAL QUALITY

Unfortunately, we have to some extent acquired a wholly artificial set of standards, which confuses function with values—a really serious confusion, leading to many misunderstandings. It would be such a good thing if we would take more note of the fact that . . . a good piece of popular music has a far better chance for what we call "immortality" than a bad symphony. . . ."

—ROGER SESSIONS

So far we have talked about musical quality in two interrelated ways. First, we developed broad concepts for evaluating music within a multicultural context, and then we talked about personal excellence as a way of life—controlling and informing everything that we do. We now need to delve into a number of issues that are bound to come up at one time or another as we make, receive, and evaluate music in a variety of circumstances.

Musical Quality and the Work of God May Be Two Separate Things

While it is true that God can speak through the mouth of a jackass (Numbers 22:21ff.) or allow the gospel to be preached out of envy (Philippians 1:15), it is not true that these are God's preferred ways of speaking. Even so, there are those who might assume that because God chooses to speak these ways at times and seemingly allows positive results to come about, they should either use, or become, jackasses themselves.

Unfortunately, many Christian music makers can behave as if God didn't care about quality. Sometimes they attempt to reach people directly out of spiritual envy. Church x, a few streets away, is having amazing success in reaching people. The congregation is growing by leaps and bounds. Programs, techniques, and numerous activities have seemingly consorted to produce something that, by golly, should be the envy of every church whose main passion is to see the world turned to Christ. And so church y, not to be outdone, copies church x.

Musical choices, technologies, and programming often play a major role in such growth strategies. These may certainly be all right in themselves. But what is not all right is why some churches try to outdo, try to keep up with, or try to mimic each other. Who is to say how large or imitative one church should get, simply because another one is growing exponentially? Who is to assume that major musical adjustments are to be made in order to bring one church up to the seeming effectiveness of another? How much of this is undertaken through the direct influence of the Holy Spirit, and how much is done because church growth looks so good that we covet it? And to what extent do excellence and musical values guide the actions? Largeness and smallness are not, in themselves, a sign of God's intervention or lack of it. They may well be signs of envy, competition, laziness, or boredom. In reality, God works through a range of quality from mediocrity to excellence. Instead of wondering why God works through mediocrity at all, we should assume that God would prefer excellence, but not at the expense of spiritual integrity. And spiritual integrity has primarily to do with why we make music, not what music we make. As much as we must strive for quality, it will not impress God all by itself. At the same time, our reasons for making music must not knowingly exclude high standards. We cannot afford to rest with mediocrity because it is effective.

Musical values should never be compromised in the name of growth, meeting people's needs, becoming or staying relevant, helping the Holy Spirit out, or the like. Good music, or aesthetic quality, must rise directly out of integrity and authenticity, and integrity and authenticity inevitably carry their own authority. It is at this point that an oft-quoted aphorism is worth repeating once more: "Holy shoddy is still shoddy."[1]

There Is a Difference Between Musical Quality and Musical Relevance

If someone honestly does not like Beethoven or, for that matter, any classical music, this is not necessarily a sign of poor taste or lack of taste. If this same person prefers progressive jazz, Islamic *maqam*, and the music of the gamelan, then the only thing that can be said is that her or his taste is different or narrowed down to other musics, but not bad. Meantime, the same thing can be said about the person who likes classical music from 1400 to 1900, John Philip Sousa, and Appalachian folk, but not much else.

In other words, it may be entirely wrong to say that musical pluralism in our present culture is legitimate only if it includes or is dominated by Western classical music. To hold to this is to imply that even though excellence can exist in other forms of music, it is derivative or contingent. So we must conclude that, given today's cultural mixes and options, including a variety of sophisticated musical types, it is entirely possible that classical music may have no relevance whatever for some people, even though they might have high aesthetic sensitivities. Or if classical music is relevant for certain people, it may not be the center. In other words, there is nothing particularly wrong about putting classical music in a less-than-primary position as long as the entirety of our musical choice is driven by a persistent desire for quality.

Consequently, we can say this: A sense of quality is preceded by a sense of musical relevance or some kind of perceptual "fit." It is only then, within perceptual fittingness, that we can address the subject of quality and taste. There is where many cultural critics and music educators get sidetracked. They assume that "great" music is not appreciated—does not fit—because people have poor aesthetic standards, instead of realizing that it may not fit because people do not find it relevant. These educators then proceed to teach "correctively," insisting on what they perceive to be good, forgetting that, most likely, they did not come to love music this way. (Remember the analogy with Romans 7.)[2] They forget that they did not begin with quality but with musical perception—which may or may not have included quality—to which issues of quality were later attached.

Production and Content Are Separate Aesthetic Issues

The performing arts (dance, drama, and music) differ from the other arts in that they are not complete until they are performed. This means two things. First, aside from recording technology, which freezes a single performance into a near infinity of exact replications, no two live performances will ever be exactly alike. And given the nature of God's way of creating, the wonder of individuated imagination and human frailty itself, this is a blessing. God's way of creating assures us that no two things are alike or will ever happen in the same way twice; individuated imagination means that no two individuals will ever do any one thing the same way; and human frailty is there to prompt us toward excellence— attempting to perform or do it better next time.

Second, it means that there are standards of quality, applying directly to performance, that are separate from the standards of quality applied to the content of the work to be performed. Hence, there is a difference between a great performance and a performance of great music. Sometimes there are great performances of great music, other times poor performances of great music, and still other times great performances of bad music. It is quite easy to confuse these, especially in a time when technique, production, and reproduction are as highly developed as they are and as important as we have made them.

It takes a long time to build up a tradition of performance excellence. This is as true of sport or craft as it is of the arts. No one will dispute the fact that, overall, there are more technically proficient performers today than ever before in the history of music making. This is both good and bad. It is good because good performance is enjoyable. As we saw in chapter 1, it is bad when the quality of the performance becomes so important that the musical content itself becomes irrelevant.[3]

There is an even more troublesome aspect to the overemphasis on production, having to do with applied technological paraphernalia, which can be used in any number of ways to enhance performance and manipulate content. In some respects, musical practice is all the better off for this. When used honestly and creatively, technological manipulation brings to music qualities and variegations that just a few years ago were only dreamed of.

In one area, however, its use should be seriously challenged. In popular music, Christian and secular, technological devices are often used to create a bigger/better-than-life environment and, even more questionably, to cover notoriously weak and untalented performers and to make even the very good artists appear to be more than they really are. This is nothing other than aesthetic cover-up. While the artistic content of live concerts can be manipulated to a remarkable degree, the real scam takes place in the recording studio, where events are so enhanced, sifted, shifted, corrected, and transformed that many artists and musical events can only survive on recordings. The ethical and aesthetic loss to young people especially is immeasurable. They have no idea of "live" authenticity and integrity. Consequently, their only option is to experience a kind of music that has no local, personal identity. The message from all of this is that their only hope, as future music makers, is to sequester themselves in a studio where they too can be enhanced and made "real." Or if they go live, they know that there is still enough equipment around to artificially transform them into what they, all by themselves, are not.

This overuse of electronic "steroids" is not only aesthetically duplicit but also unethical. It reinforces the romantic and pagan notion that artists not only are better than most people, they are Other than most. A negative synergism is built, where the whole is unfortunately greater than the sum of the parts. Dissimilarities, technological manipulation, substandard content, and questionable talent add up to a powerful delusion. The whole is not a true, organic whole; it is more like an emulsion—technically manipulated to look integrated, but patently not. And, as we know, all emulsions when left alone eventually settle into their separate layers. The same is true in the case of the technological cover-up. Things eventually settle and artists are exposed for what they truly are and technology is known for what it can only be: means.

In the Christian community, this emulsive delusion not only infects music making, but everything from preaching to corporate worship to witness. Wherever there is money, a fairly substantial inventory of electronic equipment, and people—whose theology of immediacy takes precedence over that of excellence and servanthood—there will most likely be a related show of technological force masking as the power of God, covering up questionable talent and weak content. For many, it is very hard to resist, and for others, an embarrassment.

None of this should imply that technology automatically cancels out strong content and artistic creativity. Quite the contrary. Technology and true creativity can be turned in a positive direction. What we must guard against is when technique and production are such that content, good or bad, is ignored. Means (remember, technique and technology are means) become ends, and once again we have things backward.

Musical Depth and Musical Quality

One of the aesthetic tenets of pluralism is that while quality is always an issue, it can be found in many kinds of music. The same is true of profundity. Many kinds of music can be profound, as long as we understand that there is more than one kind of profundity.

First, there is intellectually profound music, music that is structurally complex, carefully worked out, full of integrated detail, and organized into a significant architectural whole. In Western culture, this kind of profundity is found almost exclusively in classical music—not all of it, but a lot of it. This in turn calls for intellectual effort on the part of the listener and the critic who understand that the recognition and assimilation of structural process leads from surface listening to a deeper appreciation, along with enhanced abilities to provide verbal, schematic, comparative, and contextual analyses.

If we are not careful, we can assume that intellectual depth is overwhelmingly important. Then we might want further to assume that because classical music is more consciously intellectual than popular music—and by all accounts it is—popular music cannot be profound.

Three catches follow on this assumption. First, some classical music is quite devoid of conscious intellectualism, yet it is profound. Second, a significant amount of intellectually conceived music is shallow, because the only thing to take note of is its intellectual complexity. It is otherwise dry and academic—music written about music, technically complex but expressively mute. Third, popular, folk, and jazz compositions can be quite profound, even though they may be simple, short, and relatively unpolished.

The solution lies in moving beyond structural process and complexity all by themselves. Music must finally be expressively powerful, give or take intellectualism, in order for it to be truly deep. The ultimate "message," the ultimate force of any music lies in cumulative expressiveness. In other words, profundity may be of two kinds: that which is profound by virtue of its deep intellectual processes *coupled to* expressiveness, and that which probes and ponders almost exclusively *because of* its expressiveness.

Two more things. First, profundity may come out of the ability of the performer to move people deeply, either along with or in spite of the depth of the music itself. Here, we're back to the dilemma of production—now the performer—and content. Second, whenever anybody is profoundly moved by music, they should not be ridiculed, even though the music and the performance might fall below sensible standards. Their love should not be questioned; their taste, quite certainly. This is where love and patient education should always replace scolding and sneering.

Single-State Music and Musical Quality

In chapter 1 we spent some time discussing the enormous variety in God's handiwork and the implications of this for artistic and musical creativity. Consequently, the very best composers and performer/improvisers seem always to strive for a style that shows extended diversity and nuance. The total body of their music will be a mix of fast, slow, loud, soft, long, short, gentle, vigorous, brilliant, introspective, celebrative, somber, exultant, muted, multicolored, single-hued, and so on. So when we listen to the best jazz, classical, folk, rock, and popular music, we not only sense distinct stylistic differences among them but, just as importantly, varying degrees of change and variety within each of them.

By contrast, many contemporary musicians have chosen to limit their styles so drastically that the music comes off only one way. For want of a better term, we'll call this kind of music *single-state* or *single-process* music. We can particularly observe this in many of the rock substyles: acid, punk, thrash, hip hop, and house music. Rap and New Age music, in their distinctive ways, are likewise single process musics. Tempo, dynamics, beat, volume, timbre, texture, and structure are basically static and unvaried. While it may take a certain amount of creativity to get the style started up, the creativity seems to stop with the starting up. From then on, everything stays basically the same.

In the case of the rock styles, the music is not only stylistically static but abusively loud, assaultive, and in some cases physically hurtful. And it stays that way. There is virtually no subtlety, nuance, variation, ebb, and flow—it's simply "there" in its forceful changelessness. Some may contend that this music has to be this way, that is represents anger, alienation, and protest against hypocrisy, superficiality, and status quo. While this may be true in many cases, we need only refer to the Old Testament prophets, to John the Baptist, and to Jesus, all of whom showed anger and frustration in the face of similar conditions. But there is one crucial difference. They were not single-state, single-process prophets. Along with their protests and vexations, they showed meekness, quietness, and humility. They preached messages of peace and comfort, joy and celebration, and, above all, redemptive hope. It doesn't work just to be angry or vociferous, loud and aggressive. The best prophecy and the best art are multivoiced and many-sided.

Rap and New Age, while stylistically at opposite poles, are remarkably static. In the case of rap, rhythms and meters, while overt and heavy, cover very little structural distance.[4] New Age music is circularly redundant; it is changelessly unfocused and monochromatic. There is really no beginning, end, or middle. The listener can enter and exit its sound anywhere, and little is lost or gained in the process.

These musics bear a curious resemblance to a disturbing phenomenon in our culture: single-issue ideologies, interest groups, and activists disconnected from a central integrative core. When activists on any issue separate themselves from other issues, their rhetoric becomes static and fixed. In the case of single-process music, there is no variety, subtlety, or change. In the case of single-issue interest groups—despite the rightness of many of their causes—there is no central integrative moral force against which each issue could be tested and from which many of them would develop sheen, flexibility, and subtlety without losing their prophetic force. There is no shift in texture, no morally cumulative mandate, and no way of showing how creatively vigorous true morality is. In all cases, the whole is no more than the sum of its one part.

Consequently, both in the music making and the activism there is virtually no potential for greatness. Notoriety and fuss—there is an abundance of that. Nobility and nuance, near nothing. There is seemingly no concern for what it means to be fully creative, in the case of the music, or fully moral, in the case of the interest groups, for no fully creative or fully moral person should ever limit him- or herself to just the one way, just the one message, just the one state.

It is in this sense that any musical style, including the ones just spoken of, should be considered aesthetically suspect and creatively below par, even among the most tolerant pluralists.

Musical Commonness, Corniness, Mediocrity, and Kitsch

Most of us have heard of the terms high art (or culture) or low art (or culture), used to describe classical, popular, and ethnic artifacts. While we have avoided using the high/low terms so far, we are referring to them now in order to allay the suspicion that "low" or primitive art forms lack integrity, dignity, or creativity or are inherently inferior. Sometimes, there is a tendency to equate low culture and mediocrity, brought on no doubt by the very use of the word *low*.

There is a profound difference between low culture and mediocrity, and perhaps one of the best ways to explain this is by relating three terms: common, coarse, and vulgar, each in its most positive denotation.

Something can be vulgar, common, or coarse and still have integrity, worth, and aesthetic winsomeness. If we connect the three in their positive sense, we think of peasant folk, laborers, hopsacking, stews and porridges, carpenter's tools, things made with deep insight and little schooling, artifacts that show the mystery of simplicity and economy, works of art that possess dialectical and vernacular eloquence, expressions in which poetic spirit validates grammatical propriety, handiwork that shows the union of beauty, coarseness, and eloquence.

Catsup is common or coarse or vulgar, as are hash browns and onions, bratwurst, scrapple, shoofly pie, whole-grain bread, "I Wonder as I Wander," bluegrass, the blues, a cobbler's bench, thatched roofing, quilting, polkas, jigs, pie safes, Grandma Moses, hand-hewn timbers, shaped-note hymnody, and mountain dulcimers.

Béarnaise is high—haute cuisine, part of a larger elegance and finesse—as are pâté, Mozart operas, Dutch realism, silk, cloisonné, crystal, baroque pipe organs, sonnets, Shakespearian drama, Debussy, George Shearing, marquetry, L'arc de Triomphe, the cathedral of Notre Dame, ballet, classical rhetoric, and Andrew Wyeth.

Once examples such as these are listed, the differences can be seen. These are not differences in intelligence or integrity. They are brought about by intense schooling, affluence, leisure time, refinement, finely honed technique, intellectual fore- and after-thought, and, probably most of all, the integration of the finest detail with overall shape.

Three things are especially notable about these contrasts. First, many if not most of the artists and artisans responsible for the set of "high" examples, during their lifetimes, were considered much lower in station than the clientele for which their art was made. Thus in a very real sense, nearly all high quality handiwork has been made by a socioeconomically defined working class which can be divided between those who have learned to speak an artistic language of elegance and those who speak artistic languages of plainness and, for want of a better word, coarseness.

Second, despite these obvious differences, the artistic spirit always comes through and has the final word. That is, all art works, "high" and "low," in some way possess wholeness, integrity, consistency, a sense of aesthetic value—if you will, the "poetry" winning out over the "grammar," the delicate balance between over- and understate-ment, and, finally, the eloquence—the assured ability of the artifact to speak powerfully for itself even while being absorbed into the larger context.

The third matter is fascinating and, for high culture elitists, hum-bling. These two kinds of creativity have no fixed boundary between them. Their very integrity and artfulness cause them to draw from and be influenced by each other. Furthermore, high and low art pieces—and both have equal rights to this honor—rest comfortably together in museums, libraries, symposia, homes, offices, or shops. And of late, the world of academic study and criticism have done more to integrate their integrities than ever before in history. Most of us, therefore, live in a mixed world of "common" and "high" art, moving from one to the other naturally, celebratingly, and thankfully—that is, if we really care about excellence and authen-ticity. All of this is just another way of talking about the community inherent in human creativity and the elegance of brother and sister keeping.

There is a kind of music and art making, often termed "corny" (or "sentimental"), which is entirely legitimate and necessary in its place. "Corniness" is music making or letter writing or greeting card fabrication or poetry writing (and the like) that takes place in families, between lovers, among friends. It is not meant to impress or to go public but to knit and unite. In the abstract, it may be of poor quality, but seeking quality is less the point than quiet, intimate, heartfelt expression. Family sings, a grandfather getting out his cornet and playing a long-lost tune for his grandchildren, a dad whittling a boat for his boy, an aunt drawing cats and ducks for her niece, a husband writing sentimental things to his wife constitute these acts.

The reason that we are including this kind of art here is not because every creative base in the world needs to be covered but because there may be a legitimate place for it in the life of the church, as long as the church knows what it's doing and provides appropriate times and places where it acts as a closely knit family. The problem arises when corniness is formalized, made to be the ongoing thing, turned into the preferred mode, commercialized, and eventually institutionalized. And then corniness becomes embarrassing, even hypocritical.

Mediocrity and kitsch are something else altogether. And as with excellence, they know no boundaries. There is mediocre classical art and mediocre popular art. Mediocrity is simply a notable lapse of quality in any category or medium. It might be something as plausibly artistic as academic correctness without aesthetic quality, or it may be something that at every turn—structural, procedural, and aesthetic—lacks cohesion, integrity, and eloquence. Mediocrity is not easy to spot all by itself, especially for those who are just beginning to seek quality. It is best discovered when placed beside something truly good and best discussed with those who know how to teach and not scold.

Mediocrity is often the result of an aesthetic "Peter principle," the equivalent of being promoted, in business, beyond one's personal competence. That is, an artist or artisan might be very good at composing short, useful, and aesthetically pleasing works. These works consistently display an integrated sense of function and worth. Time after time the composer hits the mark. Then the Peter principle comes into play: success causes the composer to begin to out-compose his or her creative resources, to assume that large, impressive, and increasingly frequent works should be next on the agenda. The urge to be the next Brahms or Verdi overtakes a realistic sense of personal competence. But it becomes quickly apparent that the composer has risen to his or her level of incompetence. In other words, it is possible to "rise" to mediocrity by overachieving. The failure to discern this has been the degrading of many an artist.

Kitsch is mediocrity in full aesthetic masquerade. While mediocrity may be poor quality with the ring of sincerity, kitsch is presumptuous, hypocritical mediocrity; it is blatant and strident pretension. Kitsch is not lack of taste, but bad taste. Kitsch is never too little and never on time. It is intemperance and overstatement, based on a desire to imitate something really good, to work within a style but without the eye or ear for the subtle relationships among detail, nuance, and overall shape. Consequently, it barges its way through a style, using only the most obvious elements. These then become the whole, without any thought given to subtlety, detail, sensitivity, and finesse.

For example, if the artifact to be imitated is American colonial, kitsch is pseudocolonial, not semicolonial. Kitsch is the difference between an antique and "antiquing"; between crass ornamentation and subtle design; it pretends toward the whole without recognizing internal wholeness. It is surface creativity without insight. All of these attributes, it seems, arise out of an absence of authenticity. By contrast, authentic creativity imagines and crafts from the inside out, not the reverse. Creative authenticity begins with individuality and continues into an integration of the large and the small, form and shape, grammar and poetry, detail and mass. But kitsch leaps to an ideal without knowledge of what it means to slowly grow up into it. It is high culture given over to immediacy and superficial similarity. Kitsch is not artistic milk or peasant porridge but ersatz meat garnished with ersatz ornament.

The sobering thing about so much contemporary Christian music and art—all types, but especially the big-scale stuff, pseudo-symphonic, classicized popular and popularized classics, oversized choirs and instrumental groups, or, in their absence, the ever-present taped accompaniment, "excellence" in absentia—the trouble with so much of this is that it pretends so ardently, pushing for something that already exists in finer form. It is gross, large-scale, theme park imitation—inauthentic—hence so prone toward kitschiness. Without possessing an inner sense of indigeneity, so anxious to "be like," so obsessed with overstatement and so lacking in humility and meekness, it sends out the worst signals to culture about the meaning of lean, disciplined, and authentic faith. Hence, much of it is the kitsch counterpart to the musics of secular culture: the pseudoclassicisms of some, the pseudoballadry of others, the pseudofolk of still others, clean through the massive vocabularies of American music.

Entertainment and Musical Quality

Somehow it has become natural to assume that good art and entertainment are mutually exclusive. If we were given these three words—*art*, *quality*, and *entertainment*—and were asked to choose what matches and what doesn't, the most common answer would be that art and quality match and entertainment is the oddball.

This is due in part to the way critics have lined out a set of criteria that, in a sweeping gesture, assumes that entertainment is the opposite of great art. Creating high-quality art, they say, takes time, concentration, intellectual prowess, and long-term commitment. Enjoyment comes no other way. Great art is not quick and easy; it is deep and difficult. It engages us down where the real issues are, down where the sum and substance of the human dilemmas, protests, and triumphs can be found. Consequently, great art does not provide immediate gratification, nor does it court those who seek it.

Entertainment is its opposite. It lacks substance, depth, and purpose. It is fluff, whimsy, meringue, ornament. It thrives by seeking out and exploiting the lowest common denominator and proves the worth of this strategy at the cash register. Entertainment is an industry; serious art is noble purpose. Entertainment fronts for substance and seduces the unwitting into thinking that they are engaged in the real stuff of life. Entertainment is sitcom-think and Muzak; it is production over content, sizzle over substance. It is addictive—a way of "shooting up." In short, it is a sign of a civilization in its death dance.

So they say.

While there is a lot that is right about serious art and a lot wrong in the entertainment world, the picture is not all that simple. The world of so-called serious art is fraught with commercialism and superficiality. The average symphony orchestra thrives by repeating the familiar and elevating the *who* of music making over the *what* of the music. Good and less-than-good musics are often held in equal esteem because they sound alike and are given great performances by overpaid and overindulged superstars, some of whom have to be taught the music by rote. And while much of the same can be said of the so-called entertainment world, not enough is being said about the ways that excellence finds its way into a good part of its actions. Nor is enough said about the ways in which entertainment should be and is a legitimate part of all kinds and classes of music making. So the real issues do not lie in caricatured extremes of art and entertainment but in the huge expanse of perceptual territory lying in between, in which a great deal of very good music (and other kinds of art) takes place. All of this means that before a discussion of entertainment can be properly undertaken, we need to take another look at musical perception.

This is best done by describing four common perceptual scenarios in which different kinds of musical content and varying degrees of engagement with that content are combined. Two terms will be used to describe these: *deep* and *shallow*. They are not to be considered as isolated extremes but as endpoints on a continuum. Neither term carries pejorative connotations. Each is flexible and can be made to fit specific circumstances. A musical composition may be shallow from one perspective and deep from another. What may be shallow for a second grader may be deep for a college senior, and the reverse. Or elementally simple music (shallow in a musical sense) can have significant cultural impact (deep in a sociological sense). And it must be remembered that shallow need not mean trivial, mediocre, or simplistic. Rather, it can signify a completely legitimate way of approaching content, or it may refer to a type of great music.

A couple of simple analogies may help. Clean water may run shallow or deep; in either case it remains water and remains clear and clean. Milk, in the scriptural sense, is not as strong as meat. Comparatively speaking, it is shallow and meat is deep. But it is no less legitimate or complete. And for the circumstances in which the milk drinkers find themselves, it is whole, it is deep, and it is complete. Applying these analogies to music, we can say that music can be of high artistic quality and still be shallow. We can also say that music can be extremely simple and short-lived and still be deep. With regard to the former, certain fast movements of Haydn or many of the elegantly styled jazz improvisations of George Shearing come to mind. A good example of a simple and short composition of great depth is "Yesterday" by Paul McCartney of the Beatles, or the "Sarabande" from the C Minor Cello Suite by J. S. Bach. With the analogies and illustrations in mind, we can go more fully into the four perceptual scenarios.

1. *Shallow engagement with shallow content, or casual listening to elementally simple or casual music.* In this case, both engagement and musical content are light but of high quality. Here are some examples: (1) Taking in background music while watching a cartoon. The music is Bach's "Fugue a la Gigue," and the cartoon is a technologically sophisticated version of a tennis match at double speed; (2) humming "Amazing Grace" while working a precision lathe; (3) singing madrigals in a bank lobby.

2. *Shallow engagement with deep content, or casual listening to elementally complex or profoundly expressive music.* For example,

one might casually listen to a Mozart string quartet at an outdoor reception or listen to someone play a Bach trio sonata in order to determine the acoustical qualities of a new concert space or offhandedly enjoy a profound piece of music that, in other circumstances, might be engaged with deepest concentration.

3. *Deep engagement with shallow content.* Here, one may be engaged in serious study or analysis of an elementally simple composition. For instance, in Sinead O'Connor's performance of "Nothing Can Compare 2U," serious study can be given to her uncanny ability to bend, or come at, pitches from their sharp side (in contrast to the overwhelming tendency of pop musicians to bend pitches to or from the flat side). And while this is being undertaken, the same analyst could research the stylistic relationships between Irish pop/rock styles and their folk counterparts. Or, in an entirely different setting, a newcomer to an established musical style might have to concentrate deeply on a piece of music that others, familiar with the style, can take for granted. For example, a newcomer to classical music in the early stages of piano study can struggle to penetrate a mildly dissonant, technically simple composition by Béla Bartók. Furthermore, there are times when, for a variety of reasons, an admittedly shallow composition will generate deep emotional response or lead one into an engagement with profound intellectual issues that reach out beyond the music itself.

4. *Deep engagement with deep content.* This mode includes intense performance, study, or composition of structurally and expressively complex music. This is what Nicholas Wolterstorff calls perceptual contemplation.[5] While this is thought to be the normal way most people are thought—or expected—to listen to great music, it probably does not take place all that frequently. This is both bad and good.

One of the wonderful things about music—good, bad, simple, complex, shallow, and deep—is that it can be truly enjoyed and in a certain way listened to while other things go on. While there is a profound difference between music making as a coordinate of another function (harvest songs in a tribal society or singing hymns during Communion) and music making as a background to another function (Muzak in shopping malls or an organ prelude backgrounding congregational talk at the beginning of "worship"), it remains true that even the most trivial music will somehow affect a given context.

This is the good part. The bad comes when music makers and users persistently fail to approach deep content with a corresponding personal depth. In the field of classical music, there are many technically superior performers for whom profound music is just another means for demonstrating virtuosity, gathering public attention, or collecting another robust fee. There are those for whom great music has become Muzak, simply because of a perpetual habit of trivial—not shallow—engagement with meaningful content. We can call this "attitudinal Muzak." And in a culture that has become so accustomed—*addicted* is a better word—to music as *insignificant significance*, it is no wonder that even the best musical efforts, popular and classical, are often lost in the larger context of pleasurable insignificance.

The phenomenon is not limited to secular culture. Pleasurable insignificance can be sacramentalized. Trivial engagement with trivialized content, coupled to a perception that worship is pleasure and the presence of God is its chief symptom, can be easily traced to a spiritualization of insignificant significance. There is far more "Muzaking" in church music and Christian concert music than we care to admit. The example already spoken of—congregational socializing during the organ prelude—is but one example, perhaps the most minor. The larger dilemma lies in the transforming of church activities into sitcom theology, sitcom ministry, sitcom witness, and, by natural extension, sitcom music making.

As to which of the foregoing excludes entertainment, it is difficult to say, for entertainment implies engagement coupled with pleasure, at any number of levels. To say that entertainment excludes deep engagement with deep content is to overlook the more substantive and complete definition of entertainment. Webster defines entertainment as something that can be engaging as well as diverting. And even diversion can mean engaging deeply with deep content. For in addition to the diversion of pleasure, three other kinds of diversion are possible: the diversion of analysis, the diversion of association, and the diversion of worship.

1. *To analyze music as a diversion means to exchange the act of thinking in music to thinking about it.* Here the listener turns from enjoying music directly as music to a more cognitive exercise of reflecting, for example, on the process and performance of music. This could well mean that some uninformed listeners are more liable to experience music as undiluted pleasure than some educated ones are. This could further mean that there are two kinds of people who do not love music nearly as much as they could: certain educated musicians who seem to be satisfied by very little music, even though they know quite a bit about a whole lot of it, and the uneducated ones who refuse to extend their pleasure boundaries by locking themselves up into one or two kinds of music.

2. *To use association as a diversion means that music's friendliness to multiple contexts can draw the listener into contemplating, experiencing, even synthesizing the music and its widest context. The whole then becomes greater than the sum of the parts.* The listener's pleasure here is deep and rich, even ecstatic. But it is also focused, controlled, and temperate. And as contradictory as it may sound, ecstasy and temperance can actually be integrated. The apostle Paul handles this quite nicely when he speaks of singing with the mind while singing with the spirit and when he couples the ecstasies and exuberance of worship to doing everything decently and in good order. This is far different than what happens when a multitude of experiences, coming from all directions, results in insignificant significance. The pleasure derived from this can never be deep, nor can it include thoughtfulness or seriousness. It is analogous to quick sexual pleasure without love or some kind of religious fix without true worship.

3. *To use worship as a diversion means appropriately joining music making and liturgical action.* This is an even stronger way of

talking about the functional role of music in worship. The supreme worth of the one we worship demands that we be engaged in music making at the deepest level. And as we shall see in the next chapter, true worship is a complete way of life, not just an occasional foray into the sanctuary, a special feeling, or a specified sequence of events. Consequently, for the Christian, all music making—in the concert hall, in church, or at home, is a part of a larger life of worship and offering. Whether the content is shallow or deep, diversion, engagement, and pleasure are always at the deepest level, for it is the worship of God—entertaining him as he entertains us—which is the crowning glory of all our actions.

So we must conclude that entertainment can be both good and bad. It can be present in any of the deep/shallow scenarios spoken of earlier. It is a necessary ingredient of life, certainly the life in Christ. It is not out of place anywhere, even in church, as long as we know its dangers as well as its virtues. It is not the down side of a more noble action, nor does the presence of entertainment automatically mean the substitution of mediocrity for quality.

In order to discuss the dangers of entertainment, we must first of all see its value, remembering its ability both to divert and to engage, and placing these abilities alongside the four deep/shallow scenarios. We then can say that *when societies or individuals include diversion and engagement in their perceptual lives, and when quality and the pursuit of excellence drive the whole, entertainment per se can be as right as rain*. The danger in entertainment then becomes apparent. If and when an individual or society becomes *exclusively* an entertainment society; when the only and continuing object is to divert; when shallowness of content is the only allowable possibility; when easy entrance into, trivial engagement with, and easy exit from an experience dominate the whole of perceptual engagement, then we can truly say that entertainment is an evil.

With these thoughts in mind, we can begin to look around, observing churches in their worship and witness, the media engaging their publics, the arts building their audiences; gauging the direction in which money and accolades flow; sensing the intensity and direction of intellectual and aesthetic action; measuring the character and mix of public education and how it is training the perceptual capabilities of children. Then we can begin to understand how right or wrong things are, how secularized the church may or may not be. We can begin to understand to what degree a culture possesses or is losing what can only be called greatness of soul.

This last phenomenon, the trivialization of greatness, is subtle. Under the guise of the masterpiece, we perform trivial and trendy acts. We overlay trivia with *Messiah* sing-ins; we encourage the study of condensed versions of great artworks; we treat high culture as a synonym for affluence; we turn history into docudrama; we sexualize everything, which means we trivialize sex; and we thrive on familiarism—in top forty pop, top forty classical, top forty Christian contemporary, and top forty spirituality—easy entrance into, engagement with, and exit from just about everything. In a real sense, familiarism turns out to be not much more than non-engagement in all-pervasive content. And what goes around comes around.

How Can We Know? A Conclusion

So far we have talked about quality from many different angles, always assuming that it exists, knowing that it must be pursued, recognizing that pursuing it in music is but part of a larger way of life. All along we have assumed that, along with music of good quality, there is music of lesser, even poor, quality, recognizing that the very relativistic nature of music makes quality a debatable issue.

We have also tried to make it clear that while good music is to be preferred over bad music, something precedes the judging of music, namely a quality of heart and mind that goes into the making and choosing of music. We have also said that those who truly want to seek quality will find it, no matter how bereft they are initially or how slow they are in finding it in the process.

Then, we have tried to sort our way through some of the complexities that arise because we have adopted and defended a pluralistic model. And all of these things together have culminated in a discussion of the relationship between quality and appropriateness, especially in the church.

And finally, as a part of the discussion on the debatableness of musical values, we spent some time discussing the powerlessness of aesthetics to bring about changes in musical preference, unless aesthetic thought is coupled with and subordinated to actual and continual participation in music making itself. This includes the very important concept that, in addition to the immense teaching value that music inherently possesses, the best learning also demands the best teachers—committed and discerning pluralists— who have learned how to join those whom they are teaching. While they might not always like the music they join, the best teachers show love for the people who love the music they make. Thus they never take songs away from anyone. They add to them by loving, discerning, and wise mentoring. They supersede aesthetic law, with its powerlessness and its ability to take the life out of music making, by bringing their own life, their own musicking, their own celebration, their own diversity and understanding to every musical turn and condition.

But one haunting question remains, and, I must admit, it still haunts me and probably always will. *After all is said, done, taught, debated, and musicked, can we really know what quality is?* How can we really know what good music is, other than to have had our brains washed or to make all of our musical choices from a huge handed-down list of masterpieces?

Allow me to tell you how I make musical decisions. This is a lot different than telling you what musical decisions to make.

1. *Be sure that you truly want to seek and find quality with all of your heart.* Remember that seeking quality need never be at odds with the work of God, even though there are those who might make it appear to be so.

2. *Do not just think about quality; do quality. Hunt it down.* If you are not a performer in some specialist sense, remember that every time you hum a tune or sing a hymn, let alone listen to, dance to, and celebrate with music, you are a music maker. This

being so, make music actively, not just passively. Do not let music happen to you; instead, happen to it. Remember that God created you to be in charge of the creation. Be in charge when you listen to music. Otherwise you will cease to truly make music even though it is happening all around you. And you can mistakenly think that all this musical happening—this wrap-around musical environment—is the true one. It is not.

3. *Do not be afraid to pay close attention to history.* The old saying that good things will stand the test of time is a good saying. This does not mean that history is always right. Sometimes some very great musics are overlooked and sometimes some not-so-good musics are included as masterpieces. This is only because human beings make and then retell history, and human beings have ways of making mistakes. But you can rest assured that, all told, the test of time is an exemplary model for sorting quality out.

4. *Pay close attention to the experts in the field, the actual, on-the-spot music makers themselves.* Just as a gymnastic event has to be adjudicated by experts, so does musical practice. Even though the judges themselves do not always agree, we know that their disagreement is over degrees of excellence, not over excellence or mediocrity. This very debatableness, as we have seen, is part of the glory of music making. It is not as secure as measuring with a yardstick or a micrometer. Nor should it be. Music takes expert opinion, not just the ability to collect and collate musical data. Listen to these experts, and remember that they are committed to the world of excellence in a very personal and integral way. There are charlatans. This must be admitted. There are those who will put other priorities ahead of musical integrity. But, as in all other walks of life, a lack of integrity is easy to spot. And even if that lack is veneered with spirituality, tear the veneer away and see things for what they really are, because right around the corner you will find a true Christian who does music truly. Listen to her or him.

5. *Be sure that music making becomes a matter of conscience.* In the final analysis you must be accountable for every decision you

make. And even though music is not a moral quantity, its makers are morally accountable. Even though you may not be a practicing, hands-on music maker, you can begin to generate a sense of quality by combining concepts about quality with your own growing discernment. In one or two other places in the book, we have mentioned the ability of committed listeners to debate the subject of musical quality in a given genre, even though they may have had no training in aesthetic thought, musical analysis, or performance. Nonetheless, their continued and caring involvement with their musics has led them to a condition of excellence and earned them a right to participate in the larger discussion of quality. This needs to be said one more time: People who truly want to find quality will do so, no matter how long it takes or what it costs. Listeners will find themselves listening and choosing more carefully. Composers might choose to slow down and, instead of thinking of the next royalty payment, might humbly realize that they don't have that much more to say. Publishers, if they are truly honest with themselves, might have to consider retrenchment instead of lacing their catalogs with cheapened, replicative music. Pastors, church leaders, and ministers of music who truly and humbly seek quality will not only find it, but find out that God still works even when the creative process is slowed down to an honest walk, as long as it is a walk of spiritual honesty, artistic excellence, and personal integrity.

6. *Keep comparing music to music, rather than comparing music to words and spiritualized, but not necessarily biblical, comments about music.* As important as some words may be, they cannot substitute for the experience of music itself. As we saw in chapter 2, music first of all means itself. Its logic is not like the logic of speech. Its qualities are learned best through the experiences of comparative listening. Don't be afraid to begin to trust your ears.

7. *Don't make decisions about the quality of one kind of music while listening to another.* A good piece of music has a way—at the time—of impressing us with its uniqueness. When we hear Mozart, we wonder why we need Bach; when we hear Cajun, we wonder

why we need jazz; when we hear jazz, we wonder why we need rock. This is good, as long as we understand that a good piece of music is meant to bring aesthetic satisfaction, not stylistic malaise or covetousness.

8. *Avoid like the plague musical opinions that are absolutized.* And avoid musicians who have no sympathy for any music except what they like or do. They seldom teach; they can only scold. The best critics of music are those who love and sort among many kinds of music — the practicing and discerning pluralists. The worst critics are those who choose only to compare the music in question with the one kind they find acceptable.

Even though some or all of these suggestions might leave you feeling a bit vulnerable, I believe they work. They have worked for me, they are still working, and I expect them to continue. Even so, there are times when I'm not sure that I've hit a home run, but I always know that I am in the ballpark; I always know that my hunger for quality, which I hope never to forsake, keeps me in what I can only call the larger arena of excellence, an enchanting territory of musical practice: great, good, and even some fair music, but I hope no bad music.

NOTES

1. While Elton Trueblood is commonly acknowledged to have originated this remark, it has so far been impossible to document accurately.
2. See chapter 4, pp. 87–88.
3. Chapter 1, p. 28.
4. Textual content in rap does vary in content. Despite this, the rhythmic aspect of the text remains tied to the fixity of the music.
5. Nicholas Wolterstorff, *Art in Action* (Grand Rapids: Eerdmans, 1980), pp. 24–25, 34–39.

Chapter 7

THE NATURE OF WORSHIP, FAITH, GRACE, AND MUSIC MAKING

There are only three kinds of persons; those who serve God, having found Him; others who are occupied in seeking Him, not having found Him; while the remainder live without seeking Him, and without having found Him. The first are reasonable and happy, the last are foolish and unhappy; those between are unhappy and reasonable.

—PASCAL, *Pensees*

Before discussing the use of music in worship, it is important to examine the fundamental nature of worship itself. This is different than studying worship systems and liturgies. As rich and varied as they can be, they remain lifeless apart from the deeper principles that drive them. But once the nature of worship itself is understood and practiced, then everything else fits into place.

The Nature of Worship

In the most basic terms, worship consists of someone acknowledging that someone or something else is greater—worth more—and, by consequence, to be obeyed, feared, and adored.

Worship is a simultaneous expression of dependency and worth: I am unworthy; you or it are worthy, therefore worshiped (literally, *worth-shiped*). Furthermore, worship is an expression of insufficiency: I am not complete in myself; I prefer something to the point of wanting it to master me; and my preference is shown with conviction, sometimes even passion; I bow down and adore; I heed and am changed. Put another way, worship is the sign that in giving myself completely to someone or something, I want to be mastered by it.

This definition is intentionally broad because it is intended to take in the widest possible human condition. With very few changes—a few words added, deleted, or capitalized—we would have a Christian definition of worship. But first of all we have to acknowledge that the whole world, Christian and non-Christian, worships. Everyone bows down before something; everyone adores someone or something to the point of surrendering to it and being mastered by it. Sticks, stones, totem poles, jobs, circumstances, spirits, and angels—in fact, nearly all creatures—have at some time or in some place succeeded in mastering people.

A Christian worldview maintains that God, the one and only Creator, is alone worthy of worship. Recognizing that God created us in his image, it further maintains that a unique aspect of that imaging lies in the capability of the two beings to communicate with each other, to enjoy each other's presence, to love each other without end, and to be at work continually together: the one sovereignly creating, upholding what has been created and revealing himself to it, the other responding through worship, adoration, stewardly work, and creativity.

Such communion and worship are possible only because of the unique relationship between Creator and creature: the one is created in the image of the other. The difference is one of infinity and finitude: the Creator is infinitely more-than, we are finite and less-than. Even so, the relationship is based on kind: we are created in God's image. Hence worship is not a one-sided affair, the one only getting and the other only giving. True, the Creator, by his very transcendence, cannot be but worshiped. And the creature, *imago dei*, cannot help but worship. True, the worth-ship of the one naturally woos the worship of the other. But this relationship is also an exchanging of gifts, because both are givers. This is a willing union of all-sufficiency and dependence, sovereignty and subordination, prevenient love and responding love, transcendent worthiness and temporal worth. We risk a paradox: while the Creator calls for worship, the worshiper would rush to worship even if he did not call.

It is worth noting that, before Adam and Eve fell, the Scriptures do not mention worship. There would have been no need to. Only one possible relationship could spring naturally and persistently out of the union of Creator with creature, and that would have been the kind of worship described above. No other relationship could have been conceived, because there was no other person, place, or thing to be surrendered to or adored. But because of the Fall, we must talk of the worship of God in different ways because it is not natural for us to worship God, *even though it is natural for everyone to worship.*

In the most basic sense, the Fall issued in an inversion. Satan succeeded in persuading Adam and Eve that God was not more-than. Satan succeeded in making them think that they could become like God, in other words, the same-as. When Adam and Eve took Satan's advice, Satan's condition was transmitted to them. They partook of the lie and entered the inversion. In their eyes, God, the infinitely more-than, became less-than, and in God's place something else became more-than. Consequently, Adam's and Eve's dependence, subservience, adoration, and worship were turned from the one true God to a plethora of pseudogods.

Since fallenness is the result of the inversion (all lies are inversions), all non-Christian worship will of necessity subsist on this inversion. The Fall did not do away with our sense of dependency, nor did it do away with our urge to worship. Rather, it redirected it. That is, humankind continues to worship, to bow down, to surrender and be mastered, but now this worship is directed away from God toward beings that are slightly more-than (Satan, angels, and spirits), the same-as (fellow humans), or less-than (nature and human handiwork). In other words, all that is not the worship of God is idolatry because anything less than God is handiwork: spirits, humanity, the creation, and human creativity. Creature replaces Creator, slavery replaces adoration, addiction replaces hunger, blindness replaces sight, and works replace faith. To be enslaved this way and to be duped into thinking that enslavement is true freedom and worship are the final perversions of the created order. And to be hopelessly blind and deaf to this is the final outcome of a lie for which only God can be the final remedy.

A truly biblical definition of worship of necessity begins with a plan for turning the inversion right side up again. The Scriptures include or allude to just about every approach to worship there is: organized, spontaneous, public, private, simple, complex, ornate, or plain. Yet there is no comment anywhere about any one way being preferred over another. Rather, it is the spiritual condition of the worshiper that determines whether or not God is at work. This fact alone countermands the tendency to assume that if we could just find the correct or fashionably relevant system, all will be well and God will come down. This doesn't imply that we have no responsibility to make intelligent and sensitive choices or to be creative. But whatever these choices eventually are, they are incapable all by themselves of establishing the superiority of one system over another.

Three Scripture passages go to the heart of the matter. The first is Romans 12:1: "Therefore, I urge you, brothers, in view of God's mercy, to offer your bodies as living sacrifices, holy and pleasing to God—which is your spiritual worship" (NIV). In this verse, the apostle Paul is pleading for something profound and ongoing. As a summation of a lengthy, reasoned, and integrated discourse about sin and salvation (chapters 1–11), he then proceeds into an agenda for Christian living (chapters 12–15). The entire agenda is headed up by a statement about our spiritual worship. The evidence is clear: Whatever we do as Christians we do as worshipers. Verse 1 makes it clear that our worship comprises the ongoing act of being a living sacrifice—better yet, a sacrifice for as long as we are alive. What with the once-for-all sacrifice of Christ, it is no longer necessary to keep placing creatures, animals, and goods on the altar as symbols of our need for right standing. It is now our entire responsibility to become once-for-all living sacrifices because of Christ's once-for-all sacrifice for us. It is in this sense only that we can offer ourselves up completely to God.

Therefore, there can only be one call to worship, and this comes at conversion, when in complete repentance we admit to worshiping falsely, trapped by the inversion and enslaved to false gods before whom we have been dying sacrifices. This call to true worship comes but once, not every Sunday, in spite of the repeated calls to worship that begin most liturgies and orders of worship. These should not be labeled calls to worship but calls to *continuation* of worship. We do not go to church to worship, but, already at worship, we join our brothers and sisters in continuing those actions that should have been going on—privately, familially, or even corporately—all week long.

The second Scripture is John 4:23–24: "Yet a time is coming and has now come when the true worshipers will worship the Father in spirit and truth, for they are the kind of worshipers the Father seeks. God is a spirit, and his worshipers must worship in spirit and truth" (NIV). These words of Jesus were part of a winsome conversation with the Samaritan woman. During its course, the woman turned to the subject of worship, reducing the issue to one of location, environment, and time. This was no doubt due in part to the antagonism between Jews and Samaritans and certainly to her defense of the Samaritans' approach to God. After all, according to this woman, the fathers worshiped in this mountain, thus there must be something worthwhile in it all, even though the Jews maintained that Jerusalem was the preferable place. She asked Jesus what he thought of that. According to him, spirit and truth are the true domains of worship, not locations, systems, or particular times. We are free—obligated is even better—to worship as much in the workplace as in a grand sanctuary, as long as spirit and truth are preeminent. We worship *in* spirit and *in* truth, of which preludes and fugues, art pieces, grand architecture, stained glass, or cleverly orchestrated activities are only evidences. This worship does not just contain truth; it is *according to* truth.

Psalm 29:2 is the third Scripture. It begins with a commandment to ascribe (impute, attribute) glory to the Lord, which is "due to His name." This commandment is followed by another one to worship

God in the beauty of holiness. Once again, we are brought face to face with the reality of worship as an ongoing state. Whereas the passage in Romans describes worship as a continued personal offering up and the passage in John shows that worship is to take place irrespective of location or circumstance, the Psalms passage locates worship within a continuing condition of life. The beauty of holiness—not the holiness of beauty or the equation of spiritual cleanness with aesthetic rightness—is a state to which we are called immediately at conversion, a state to which and from which we work out our salvation daily (Philippians 2:12), a state outside of which no one can see the Lord (Hebrews 12:14).

Our worship is not just the occasional and ceremonial, even sincere, worship of a holy God, but a striving after personal and continuing holiness, following hard after Christ, imitating him. This is not a dichotomized holiness, separating the sacred and secular, church and workday. It is the holiness of the twenty-four-hour day, the state of being saved, of continuing as a living sacrifice, led by the Spirit in the arena of truth. This is not the holiness of occasional worship separated away from ordinary activities. This is the only way of worship: from new birth to and throughout eternity, irrespective of time, place, circumstance, system, protocol, and handiwork.

Only after we understand what true worship really is are we free to study and draw from the vast assortment of worship styles and activities that are available. Then we can understand how often we succumb to worshiping worship or worshiping about worship. We can understand the weakness of specially planned "worship" events, set apart from other spiritual events. And we can understand that no amount of methodologizing brings true worship into being. Finally, we will discover that much of what we call worship may only be manipulation, self-consciously contrived and depending more on conditioned reflex than faith: works lording it over faith, production more important than content, and addiction preempting mystery, faith, and newness.

If we are to offer ourselves up for as long as we have being; if this offering up is accomplished in spirit and according to truth; and if the condition in which this is to be done is one of continuing personal holiness, it follows logically that for the true Christian, all of life, not just fractions of it, is a continuum of action upon action, faithfully and knowingly made into offering after offering. *Therefore, all things done, whatever they comprise—all work, all handiwork, all of everything—can only be one act of worship after another. True worship is to love God so much that an offering is the only possible action, even though a world full of such actions can never suffice. So while it is entirely possible for Christians to worship truly without music, it is impossible for them to make music truly without worshiping.*

Worship and Musical Action: Acts, Tools, or Aids

How does music "work" in worship? Some say that it, and the rest of the arts, are aids to or tools of worship. The idea of music as a tool may sound good at first, because all of us want to worship and if anything can help us achieve that end, so much the better. But if the principles described in the first section make any biblical sense, music cannot be a tool. There we said that the Christian, already at worship, is responsible to act, to make offerings of music, instead of waiting to be acted upon by it. And this concept is not limited to a musical performance itself, but to every action leading up to it: choosing, practicing, revising, correcting, even beginning all over again.

Likewise, music making is no more limited to churchgoing than worship itself is. The psalmist puts it this way: "I will sing unto the Lord for as long as I have being." Whether an act of worship issues in creating something as long-lasting as a building or as transient as a musical performance; whether the offering is simple or complex, well done or not so well done; whether it is African, Indonesian, or American; whether it takes place in a church or a kitchen or a concert hall; if it is made with all of our heart and might and offered to God by faith, it can be nothing less than an act of worship. Then, according to Psalm 22:3, God both inhabits the offering and is enthroned upon it.[1]

The same goes for hearing music. Listeners are co-offerers. The performer offers the performance, the listeners offer their hearing. In other words, an offering is not something spectated or merely audited; all worshipers are at work worshiping. On a Sunday morning, the organist offers the prelude. The persons in the pew, at worship before they have taken their places there, make an offering of what they hear, whether the offering is loud or soft, simple or complex, familiar or strange, liked or disliked. The issue is not whether the music has merit or power, but whether the worshipers are making an offering. If they can't worship until the right music comes by (and what if it doesn't?), then they are essentially preferring the gift to the giver, or making God's presence contingent on the quality or effect of the gift.

Music and art are not messiah. They are not Holy Spirit. They are not means and they are not end. Only God is means; only God is end. It is our responsibility to take faithful action and to continue our worship at all times and in all places.

The idea that music is a tool of worship can be debated from another angle. A tool is designed to accomplish a task or to get something done. A hammer drives nails; a lathe shapes metal; a scalpel cuts flesh. Tools can even be used to make other tools. If we say that the arts were one large set of tools, making worship possible, then what artistic acts comprise worship itself? If the Scriptures call upon us to worship the Lord *with* singing, dancing, and instruments of music, then how can we worship *with* something that has previously been designated as a means for bringing worship about?

Let's go further. If we say that the arts are tools for worship, then the arts can only precede worship. Accordingly, this cuts worship down to praying, preaching, and hearing the Word of God. But isn't singing a form of praying or proclamation? And isn't it Word centered? What is a sermon, then, an act of worship or an aid to worship? Returning to Romans 12:1, if everything done constitutes a life of worship, where do the tools fit in? If they are devices for bringing this continuum about, then they lie outside of or come before worship. If this is so, then part of our lives is nonworship, and the tools are preworship. By contrast, true worship comprises all its actions and all of its pieces, the whole greater than the sum of the parts.

"Well and good," you might say, "but I still have to reckon with my feelings when I hear music. It moves me, sometimes very deeply. Whatever you say theologically about worship being a lifelong continuum of actions, I must say that when I hear a certain piece of music, there is no doubt in my mind that I am drawn closer to the Lord. Somehow when I hear music I am able to commune with God better than if I were not to hear it. In short, music enhances my worship." This may be true, but keep in mind the following:

Being emotionally moved by music is not the same as being spiritually or morally shaped by it. Those who love God and desire to worship but have not yet come to the more biblical understanding that worship is a continuing state will quite naturally cleave to any action that moves them emotionally and approximates a sense of worship itself. But being drawn to God this way by music almost always depends on music that they already know. Remember that to worship God freely is to be free of the offering; so free, in fact, that being moved or not being moved by it is irrelevant. This is the same as exercising the kind of faith that Hebrews 11:1 so succinctly describes. Admittedly, such a concept introduces the concept of work—vigorous work, the opposite of passivity—into worship. But it is the kind of work that follows hard after faith. It is the work of Christians trained for action, trained for sojourn, prepared to step out in the spirit of Abraham, not needing to know where they are going, believing God and, all along, being counted as righteous.

All true acts of worship are linked to, and supportive of, further acts of worship. One action breeds another action. This idea is distinct from saying that an aid to worship leads to an act of worship. Connecting acts of worship to further acts of worship protects against the idea that there is some sort of high point to worship. Quite the contrary; there is no predictable and hierarchical high point in true worship. If there is such a thing it will come, not of its own, but from God alone, at any time, in any place, to one or to all.

Music-as-aid is a different matter for the believer than for the nonbeliever. That is, living by faith is substantively different than living by works. Once they are saved, Christians must immediately proceed from works causing faith to faith growing into more faith, from milk to meat, and from nowness to nextness. They should not continue to behave as if they are to be led back *into* faith again and again, looking back, expecting something to lead them into worship the same way that they were led into the faith.

Being moved by music is secondary to worshiping God. The Spirit is always to be free to direct our worship, whether the music moves us or not. It is only when being moved by music is coupled to a *preceding* passion for God that we are truly moved. Behind all of this is the Lord's continuous invitation to come and to continue worship. God wills that all of us worship him. Behind all of these secondary movings—music, art, drama, dance, architecture, atmosphere, and environment—is the primary mover, whose most quiet call and gentlest reminder speak louder than our most elaborate art pieces.

Aesthetic excitement, at whatever level and from whatever source, is as much a part of being human as loving is. Ecstasy is, in itself, an offerable act. So instead of assuming that worship is the same as ecstasy, we must assume that if we do become ecstatic, this emotion itself is to be offered up as an act of worship, instead of being substituted for or equated with it. The danger lies in assuming that ecstasy is a prerequisite of worship or equal to it. Aesthetic ecstasy is, quite simply, aesthetic ecstasy. The importance of aesthetic ecstasy for the worshiper is that it should take place within an already ecstatic heart, made that way by the overwhelming love of God, whether music is present or not.

Faith and Musical Action

True worship is not possible without faith. Faith is absolute trust in the one true God who is to be believed for everything he has said and done. Other kinds of faith are either wrong or secondary. They are wrong when they make ultimate anything or anyone other than the one true God. They are secondary, as in the case of having faith in another human being or trusting the safety of a suspension bridge. Secondary faith is necessary in our everyday living. It facilitates a good part of living and it tests the presence or condition of our primary faith. But it becomes wrong when it takes the place of primary faith. Christians are instructed to examine themselves to see if they are in the faith (2 Corinthians 13:5), not raising secondary faith to a primary level or reversing faith and works.

Music, in this respect, has no more or no less importance than plumbing, piloting, parenting, carpentry, and garbage collecting. Bach's *Mass in B Minor*, in all of its magnificence, beauty, and power, has no more earning power before God than garbage collecting. Even though some would agree that garbage collectors are more socially necessary than musicians, this does not mean that collecting garbage brings one nearer God than singing Bach does. There is a profound difference between great music activating our spirit and our truly being in the Spirit. Works can quite legitimately and easily initiate the former, but only faith can initiate the latter. It is in this sense that Christian musicians must be particularly cautious. They can create the impression that God is more present when music is being made than when it is not; that worship is more possible with music than without it; and that God might possibly depend on its presence before appearing. Faith, in its proper scriptural definition, does away with these errors without doing away with music. It puts music in its proper place, along with every other act and offering: giver before gift and worship containing, not being contained by, acts of worship.

Faith must be at work another way, by causing the familiar to become new again and the new to become near and familiar. The danger of the familiar, all by itself, has already been spoken of in chapter 1. Yet a good portion of our living and our worship contains repeated actions: prayers, creeds, Scripture portions, music, art pieces, liturgies, and orders of worship. Life is delightfully full of repetitions, and we need them as much as we need complete newness, provided we keep the principle of faith at work in each repetition. Otherwise, we become guilty of vain repetition.

Faith also makes strange things near and familiar. To live by faith is to learn to welcome the unseen and the unknown, to weave it into the commonplace. Christians are the only ones on earth truly equipped to encounter the unfamiliar and to do so with rejoicing, without confusion, without bafflement, or without worshiping newness for its own sake.

Because true Christianity cannot be thought of apart from new creation, there should be no kind of music, however radical, however new, however strange, that is out of place in Christian worship, *as long as it is faithfully offered. And no Christian, truly living by faith, should ever turn his or her back on and refuse to offer a musical piece simply because it is too radical.* This is far different than saying, "If I can't figure it out, I can't offer it" or "I remember this from past Sundays, therefore I worship."

Christian music makers have to risk new ways of praising God. Their faith must convince them that however strange or new an offering may be, it cannot out-reach, out-imagine or overwhelm God. God remains God, ready to stoop down in the most wonderful way, amidst all of the flurry and mystery of newness and repetition, to touch souls and hearts, all because faith has been exercised and Christ's ways have been imitated. Meanwhile, a thousand tongues will never be enough.

There are two ways we can pray, one when we are surrounded by the familiar, the other in the middle of newness:

"Almighty God, here I am again in the same place, hearing the same music. I love it; it means much; I feel close to you and know you to be close to me. Help me to understand that I risk danger by vainly repeating, by assuming that you are nearer because everything is so familiar. Instead, make all of this new to me once again, as only the God of all mystery can. Take me back to the first day of creation when all was new; bestow on me the gift of offering all to you as never before."

Or:

"Almighty God, what I am now seeing and hearing makes no sense. It is not what I like or what I expected. Even so, it is here; I am here; you are here. There are some here who passionately love you and have made this offering to you, even though I can't make hide nor hair of it. Nonetheless, I join with them by faith; I join with an offering that, to me, only bespeaks a mystery. I offer what I do not understand to you, the one whom I will never fully understand. I gladly add one more tongue to my fallible and limited repertoire of praise. I pray that when this strangeness that I am now experiencing turns out to be familiar, I will remember the first time, the strangeness and the newness. And I also pray that as this new thing becomes familiar, I will be on the lookout for something yet to come, something ever new. I turn from what I already know to what I need to know. I worship by faith and faith alone."

This discussion is not complete without a few words as to how God looks at our music making. All along it has been assumed that music making is an offering to God; that as musically magnificent as the offering might be, it has no special merit; and that the condition of the offerer's faith takes precedence over the time, circumstance, and quality of the art. There is only one way to God, through Jesus Christ, author and finisher. All sacrifices, living and inanimate, are saved to the uttermost when they come to God through Christ. This means that God sees and hears all of our offerings, perfected. God sees and hears as no human being can, all because our offerings have been perfected by the giver. The out-of-tune singing of an ordinary believer, the hymnic chant of the aborigine, the dance of a Barishnikov, the open frankness of a primitive art piece, the nearly transcendent "Kyrie" of Bach's *B Minor Mass*, the praise choruses of the charismatic, the drum praise of the Cameroonian—everything from the widow's mite to the poured-out ointment of artistic action—are at once humbled and exalted by the strong saving work of Christ. While the believer offers, Christ perfects. It is all of Christ and it is all by faith.

Finally, faith is only unto faith. Just as we worship while continuing to worship, are saved while being saved, believe while being visited with unbelief, and sin while being forgiven, we are to exercise faith unto faith, not faith unto something other than faith. We offer our music by faith unto an increase in faith, knowing that God hears and is delighted; knowing that faith will sometime be turned to sight; and that we will finally know as we are known.

God's Grace and Music Making

When we speak of God's grace, we find ourselves in that same dilemma of wanting to say all that it means and how it interconnects and finding ourselves searching for words. So we return to tried-and-true statements, ones that describe grace as inexhaustible benevolence. This benevolence comes directly to us, unconditionally and freely given, unearned and undeserved. It is divinely contrary to our finite versions of favoritism and legalism. Grace is God's way of showing that divine initiatives are not grudging, preferential, or limited. Rather, they are loving, cleansing, anointing, lavish, and redemptive. God freely bestows the fullness of his goodwill on those who may not only be unaware of it but even resentful. Even so, grace flows: free grace, saving grace, gifting grace, enabling grace, providing grace, abounding grace, and strengthening grace. The grace of God can be no better described than in these statements: "In this is love; not that we loved God, but that He first loved us and sent His Son to be the propitiation for our sins" (1 John 4:10); "But where sin increased, grace abounded all the more" (Romans 5:20); "My grace is sufficient for you, for power is perfected in weakness." (2 Corinthians 12:9); "For of His fulness we have all received, and grace upon grace" (John 1:16, all NASB).

God's grace is not for the select few, for the especially redeemed. It does not come to us after we turn to God, but precedes, surrounds, and enables our turning. God's grace precedes our entire condition simply because God *is* grace (just as God *is* love). And because God is unchanging, because God has no favorites as to race, class, or condition, God's grace remains the same for us—free to receive or refuse it—as for Noah, Abraham and Sarah, Saul, David, Judas, Paul, Luther, Wesley, Hussein, Mother Teresa, carpenters, criminals, nurses, generals, plumbers, mothers, prisoners, secretaries, and college presidents.

Music and grace are most powerfully interconnected at the point of redemption. This can be seen in the following ways.

1. *God's saving grace produces songs in the hearts of the redeemed.* The Psalms repeatedly speak of singing of God's salvation. The apostle Paul speaks of the instructing songs of the church; that is, he instructs the church to pass grace along, singing from grace to grace, through music making. Grace is passed instructionally through the text, which is celebrated musically as corporate offering to God. Paul talked of "singing and making melody in your hearts to the Lord." Through and through, the redeemed of the Lord are inevitably led to music making—singing of the ways of the Lord.

2. *The Scriptures speak of God rejoicing over his children with singing (Zephaniah 3:17).* At one level, those who are graciously saved respond to the Savior with song. Meanwhile, the all-gracious and eternally saving Father sings *over* those who are singing *to* him. What this divine singing is like no one can imagine. It is as unfathomable and irresistible as grace itself. It springs out of grace, it is driven by redeeming love and consummated in the victory of Christ, and it results in the songs with which the church graces its praise.

3. *The final triumph of grace will issue in the music of the new heaven and earth.* The book of Revelation spends no little time on the eternal songs of the redeemed. The church, singing of the grace of God—having triumphed through Jesus Christ—continues the song begun on earth but now unimaginably transformed by the very power that takes full responsibility for the new creation. The eternally gathered church will finally hear the triune God singing

over the entire creation; it will hear the bridegroom, Christ, singing over his bride, the church. Grace, in its final uninhibited triumph; faith having turned from trust to sight; and worship having been totally purified—these together will generate an endless song of which no one presently can give full account.

4. *Grace is not just something we keep to ourselves, a privately glorious favoring. We sing of God's grace; we play of God's grace to the whole world.* We do this two ways. First, the church tells of God's grace through song. Call these songs what you want—gospel songs, hymns, chorales, choruses, and chant. If a good portion of them do not carry direct messages of grace and the remainder do not point to grace through other scriptural messages, then the church fails its musical task. Second, music itself, with or without words, is its own kind of grace. It is ointment poured over the feet of the Savior, a sweet ministry to ears, to souls, and to lives. Christian musicians, while delivered of the fixation that there is an exclusively Christian music, know of the larger graciousness of all good music. They know of the obligation to make music as agents of God's grace. They make music graciously, whatever its kind or style, as ambassadors of Christ, showing love, humility, servanthood, meekness, victory, and good example.

The days are over when music making is considered to be a part of a larger expiatory action, part of a collection of strenuous works intended to placate, to move, to pay off God—not a God of love and grace but aloofness and reluctance; not a God of faith but of frantic works. Music is freely made, by faith, as an act of worship, in direct response to the overflowing grace of God in Christ Jesus.

NOTES

1. The New American Standard Bible reads "enthroned"; the King James reads "inhabitest."

Chapter 8

THE WORLD OF CHRISTIAN
POPULAR MUSIC

The melody makes the song, not a loud noise.

—FRENCH SAYING

Make a joyful noise unto the Lord.

—PSALM 100:1 (KJV)

While Christian contemporary music (CCM from now on) is immensely popular—it may well be *the* preeminent music of American evangelicals, if not even a larger Christian population—and while it may exert enormous influence on the musical life of the church itself, it is much more than church music. It is, above all, part and parcel of the massive phenomenon of American popular culture. It is inextricably linked with it in ways that go beyond the Sunday-by-Sunday stuff of congregational song, anthems, special music, instrumental preludes and postludes, and praise choruses. These may be influenced by CCM, but they cannot be fully equated with it.

Before going further, we need to clarify what is meant by two of the three words in the CCM label: *Christian* and *contemporary*. First, the term *Christian*. As we have already discovered, *Christian* can only apply to textual content. The musical styles of CCM are neither Christian nor non-Christian. They are simply music. CCM artists may or may not be Christians. This is not to cast doubt on any of them but to concede the very possibility that non-Christians can play and sing Christian music and do a very good job of it. For that matter, it is common practice among CCM artists to employ studio musicians without screening them as to their beliefs and lifestyles. Nonetheless, we must remove ourselves from the dangerous business of being judges. This being said, it remains clear that the overall intention of CCM is to be Christian, both as to textual content and the witness of the artists themselves.

Second, the term *contemporary* simply means "(along) with the time," or "at the time of." In this sense, it is an accurate label for the body of current popular musical styles that CCM is "along with." "Contemporary" and "new" are not the same thing. "New" implies innovation, breaking fresh ground that, especially in the world of music and art, demands experimentation and not a small amount of risk. CCM, by paralleling what is already musically happening, is both "contemporary" and musically conservative. Seen this way, the phenomenon of CCM is less one of "what's new" than "what's preferred."

Toward an Overview of Popular Culture and the Electronic Media

CCM is a part of the national youth culture and thus intimately tied to the electronic media. In the words of the authors of *Dancing in the Dark*, a book that explores the relation of media and youth culture, "Without the electronic media there would not be a youth culture as we now know it." The youth culture is not autonomous, influencing and directing its own course of events. Rather, the media "have continuously reformulated the youth culture according to the latest trends in clothing, language, leisure activities, technology and especially electronic media consumption, which has . . . attempted to read the tea leaves of social and cultural change in order to capitalize on the hungers and discontents of youth."[1]

In this way, the media serve as "gatekeepers" and the process of "gatekeeping,"[2] by which a series of agents, concert promoters, record producers, artist and repertoire developers, record companies, radio station programmers, deejays, and purchasers for owners of record stores and chains screen all but a small number of potential stars. This has two effects on the youth culture. First, it controls what the youth culture sees and hears. While the youth culture perceives itself to be choosing freely, in reality it is not, for it cannot choose what it never becomes aware of.

Second, gatekeeping influences new musicians working in garage bands and playing local concerts and dances. If these musicians are fortunate enough to land a recording contract, they must then subject themselves to the designs of the gatekeepers. Thereafter, whatever the band plays, wears, says, and does is subject to the gatekeepers. [3]

It is in the context of this mixture of marketing and determinism that the concept of electronic intimacy emerges. The difference between the original garage band and the media-distributed one is not so much a matter of musical content and style. It is more the capability of the media for creating "special 'relationships' with youth, bonds which then establish allegiance . . . a feeling of closeness, sometimes bordering on intimacy, between media celebrities and individual viewers and listeners."[4] Capitalizing on young people's desires to seek meaningful intimate relationships, the entertainment industry exploits this fabricated intimacy by using the stars and entertainers to endorse and advertise products. This ensures that young people will link their identity to that of the entertainers, mimicking the way they dress, talk, and behave. Furthermore, it is readily apparent that the gatekeepers, agents, and purveyors continually improve their ability to mask the fabrication and to make fabricated intimacy appear all the more real.

This results in two especially harmful conditions that serious educators, social critics, and communication theorists have all agreed upon for some time, and what the authors of *Dancing in the Dark* correctly identify, as the dilemma of "locale and identity." First, there is confusion of place. While young people physically inhabit homes, schools, malls, and perhaps churches—eating, sleeping, studying, socializing, and doing occasional religious things—their existentially "real" locale, the place where their "authentic" sense of being and identity are created, is largely fabricated by their connection to the stars of the electronic media.

This latter world, artificially near, artificially intimate, is where the supposedly real connections are made and where the working values are shaped.

Meanwhile, what happens at home, in school, and at church is contingent on and interpreted by what the young people bring to it from the fabricated world that opens up to them by way of their electronic receivers. The real, nearby people—peers, parents, teachers, and church leaders, the ones with whom authentic face-to-face relationships could be possible and from whom example and support could come—seem too small, too insignificant, not with it. There are not enough acceptable local heroes or mentors, too few relevant, down-to-earth examples. Some try to overcome this problem by adopting the ways of mediaspeak and trying to "get down" with the young. The result can be pitifully artificial and insincere, and most young people see straight through it. These local substitutes simply cannot keep pace with the technologically polished super figures whose real personhood is hidden and whose values—whatever they are—are likewise hidden. The intimacy, so desperately needed by young people, turns out to be ephemeral. In the end, no one is really or fully there.

Second, the electronic media are saturated with performers whose only seeming objective is to draw *from* their audiences while ostensibly giving *to* them. This is cleverly disguised, of course, by the sheer force and opulence of the performance itself, being made to appear as if it was really created for the sake of the audience. The performers seem to be hard at work—energized, intense, and seemingly always "up" for the show—but their object is less one of forging a communal link with the audience than drawing the audience up into their own ego.

This takes the dilemmas of fabricated intimacy and locale and identity all the further. While young people may feel that they are connecting, being authenticated by, and identified with the performers, they are not only being sucked up into ego needs of the performers, they are also being subtly taught how to crave this same kind of attention themselves. Thus the performers and the audiences are united by a common question: "What is this doing for me?" Two credos result, the first for the entertainer: *The crowds worship me, therefore I am*; the second for the young audiences: *We imitate the entertainers, therefore we are.*

The world of mass culture and the electronic media subsists on images, set in the context of a loss of moral center and the death of meaningful language. This is the world of spin doctors, sound bites, lip synching, applause and laugh tracks, fabricated ambiguity, doublespeak, and technospeak. In this environment, the lines between entertainment and important social and political functions become increasingly blurred.

Media stars are employed to make political statements and politicians may rise or fall on their ability to appear as media stars. News reporting is a world of images and image building. Commentators and reporters are hired and retained on their ability to make ordinary news into something larger than it is—to search, in fact, for the right kind of news and to shape it so that it becomes more than useful information. Investigative reporting, docudrama, and talk shows have become strangely alike. People in the news—the serial killers, the darlings of social event, media stars, and world power figures—are all on stage. Their actions are blurred into the stuff of the news plot and the news plot is blurred into the stuff of the docudrama. Television commercials, for so long the bane of programming, have in many instances become more theatrically interesting than the programs they interrupt. They manipulate by making artificial images appear to be real, useful, and desirable. The sum of it all is that mass culture has settled down into a rhythm of electronic voyeurism, peering into war, rape, discontent, scandal, pseudoissues, scam, and an occasional tidbit of joy.

Televangelism and, for that matter, a good amount of local church life, are not all that different. Sitcom religion, theology as docudrama, and liturgy as showcasing often participate in the dilemma. Ordinary church life—preaching, praying, and singing—is turned into showboating and liturgical drama into the equivalent of the Brady Bunch. These then make a sham out of the use of true drama in worship. And the church may provide its own brand of image making, sound (read truth) bites, and theological spins on ordinary things. Spiritual matters, especially those that are heavily experiential, can slip over into the artificially dramatic and theatrical. And quite often the pulpit is where some of the heaviest image making—carefully tailored and rehearsed—can take place. On the religious talk show, the stage is set, the props are there, along with theme park reality—kitsch—a part of the greater phenomenon of American mass culture as one gigantic image, a huge docudrama, in which the lines between reality and fantasy, between truth and spin are increasingly blurred.

Wherever we look—for we are a looking society—we are faced with some kind of show, an off-brand theater, a denigration of true theater and sensible reality. It is not true theater because it is contrived to manipulate, to relativize, to hide and disorient reality, to mask the substantive, to diffuse the truth and relativize the ethical. Television is the great center, not of ideas but images or, at best, ideas blurred by images and technique. The end result is that most of contemporary society, overwhelmed by the power and presence of the media, lives in a generic world of contrived subjectivity and commercially driven pseudoreality, in which spin—long or short, simple or complex—is of the ongoing essence.

CCM: Issues and Questions

CCM as an industry is not easily separated from the larger procedural workings of the electronic media. Whatever else it is, CCM is business, promotion, advertising, marketing, technology, technique, populism, and, musically speaking, virtual parallelism to secular pop. However, for the most part CCM remains pretty much true to the textual content of its many musical styles, as well as the on- and off-stage behavior of its artists. Thus while there may be almost complete identity with the secular electronic media as to musical content and commercial process, there is a noticeable and often prophetic separation from these media where truth is rightly to remain truth. The most authentic CCM artists prove this time and again.

We must examine, however, the extent to which Christian music has separated itself from that of the church instead of separating itself from that of the world. While CCM endorses the idea that the only viable styles are those of secular culture, the churchly styles—not just the stuffy, academic music, but the splendid heritage of two thousand years—are suddenly suspect. When the Christian's most noticeable music is so stylistically and procedurally identified with the very culture it sets out to confront, something—far deeper than the musical actions themselves—is wrong. The problem is not CCM's capability for witness. By all accounts, it witnesses in some way. The problem is its capability to witness *completely*—not just about Jesus' power to begin the new birth, but to continue it, to confront souls and worldviews so forcefully that one of two things must happen: culture is transformed or it simply walks away, unrelenting and unrepentant, just as it happened with those who encountered Christ himself.

In all of this discussion, we must keep reminding ourselves that we are not talking about whether music is Christian or non-Christian. I hope that issue has been laid to rest. Rather, the question is one of doing music christianly. And this means that biblical principles, driving a thoroughly Christian worldview, drive the music makers and their music making.

CCM: Electronic Intimacy, Fabricated Intimacy, Locale, and Identity

Both Christians and non-Christians take notice of CCM. To the Christians, CCM artists are just about everything that secular artists are: idols, famous, charismatic, role models, examples, and trend-setters for irrelevant church music. To the non-Christian, the lyrics and the lifestyles of CCM artists may turn out to be life changing or remain simply a moral wrinkle in the larger cloth of popular music, much the way gospel music is currently perceived. The music is still the music.

Many young Christians who listen to CCM continue to listen to secular pop in almost all of its vocabularies, with one or more styles of rock being central. If they have a concern, it will be mostly with the lyrics rather than the music. Either they tune them out while enjoying the music (often not without a tinge of guilt), or they find music with good lyrics.

This can only mean that they are bound to participate in the larger ethos of the electronic media. Electronic intimacy, fabricated intimacy prescreened by gatekeeping, guides their perceptual mechanisms. While their Christianity may furnish them with a kind of perceptual cushion, and while the lyrics and lifestyles of CCM are no doubt meaningful to them, there is very little doubt that they are still blown away by Christian x's light shows, y's fame, and z's sound system. There is still that awestruck, wide-eyed wonder, groupiness, and distance that is found in the secular arena. And there may be more electronic fabrication, fabricated intimacy, and disruptions of locale and identity then we care to admit.

But in all fairness, there may be some differences between CCM and secular pop. Young people see CCM artists as fellow Christians, soul mates, and, in a special way, the saviors of pop music who validate Christianity—run interference—for them. CCM artists are champions, not just idols. By doing what they do, they legitimize pop and further demonstrate that it may just be possible for Christians to make it past the gatekeepers. But this question lingers: Is the larger perceptual power and distancing of the electronic media so overwhelming that for CCM this intimacy turns out to be just as fabricated and mythological as the rest?

Concerning the issue of locale and identity, CCM may hold a slight edge. It is probably true that more young people listen to CCM because they have come to Christ (or because it is part of a Christian environment) than those who come to Christ because they have listened to CCM. Furthermore, Christian young people may be able to relate more meaningfully to local contexts. While there certainly are perceptual, moral, and emotional disjunctions at home and church, Christian young people have more opportunities to address them in Sunday school, youth groups, and even at home.

And while electronic intimacy and fabricated intimacy are a real possibility, it may be that local youth leaders and directors of youth music may be able to serve as intermediate mentors—proxies, if you will—for the CCM artists. Granted, this is a lot to assume, but the degree to which they are "cool" and "with it" may determine the extent to which problems with locale and identity, electronic and fabricated intimacy are at least partly ameliorated.

But this may not eliminate the deeper issues inherent in the relationship of CCM to the world of the electronic media. Many CCM performers still become media myth figures—distant and larger than life—and as such absent themselves from the contexts of locality. They may not be truly near, truly intimate, and personally related to their young listeners. If the true role of CCM is in any way connected to ministry, then the trappings of stardom, commerce, and personal distance can stand directly in the way. There is a profound difference between a nearby role model and a distant media hero. And which do young people need most?

As mentioned earlier, one of the realities of electronic and fabricated intimacy, in addition to its being artificial, is that it is almost entirely one-dimensional. Young people get to see only that part of the artist making only that one kind of music in that one personal style in those singular concert sites or media appearances. Whizbang production and musical quantity are designed to give the impression that the audience is seeing and hearing a complete person, when it is really a carefully screened and edited "slice" of that person. This slice is contrived to look whole, as if this is what the artist's life is all about. The message from the performers to the audience is subtle but strong: "What you see and hear is what we really are. There is no need for more." The artists may or may not want it this way, but that is the way the media work, and that's what gatekeeping, image building, and fabricated intimacy produce. The whole person is hidden, separated away from the everyday, the commonplace, and the real. Only the public slice is revealed. The net effect is the opposite of artistic diversity and personal wholeness.

Ultimately this can be provincializing. As to musical practice and preferences, the message is: Stay narrow; do it my way. For there is no way for the artist to show that he or she may be wholesomely pluralistic, because the only musical message that gets out comes from that one musical slice. In other words, media fabrications preclude integrative teaching. Pop and CCM artists have no opportunity to tell young people about the values of musical pluralism, including classical music, even though these might be a regular part of their musical lives. As a result, young people are given the impression that musical breadth and variety are square. But in the meantime, they are being made into squares by those who can only show the media-hyped and limited slice.

So the real problem for CCM stars is one of breaking out of the slice—if they are personally capable of that—and into corporate and musical wholeness, in order that they can become more than media-shaped, single-music, one-dimensional role models. Admittedly this is a problem for artists of any genre. Classical musicians, for example, can be guilty of creating their particular slice and limiting people's sense of musical option. But there is one interesting difference between CCM and classical music. Most young people who love classical music—and this includes a significant portion of the most serious music majors—also enjoy CCM and other popular music. And the same goes for many classical artists as well. But the reverse is not nearly as true. In other words, "high culture," as much as it is criticized for its snobbery and aloofness, diversifies and crosses over into popular culture with an ease and tolerance that popular music and musicians seldom show for classical music. Therefore, if CCM artists want truly to encourage artistic freedom and musical pluralism, they must emerge from their narrow musical slice and more effectively demonstrate how wide the world of music really is. Otherwise, they join company with the very provincials and reactionaries whom they often condemn for not accepting CCM.

We can take the one-slice idea further. One of the most sociologically questionable aspects of the star system, particularly the kind created by the electronic media, is that it so completely segregates the talented from the ordinary. Once talent, however the gatekeepers define it, is discovered, it is removed from the very community—the local contexts—of which it was once a part. A slice is taken and placed "out there" in another dimension, out of personal touch. Slicing talent out of the community is a direct challenge to the fundamental and biblical concept of community, in which giftedness is simply a part of the continuum of giving, sharing, influencing, and being influenced by the gifts of others. This is an issue that the entire world of art should face more squarely. But the very nature of *Christian* music making demands an even more radical response.

In short, artists can choose how far they want to go into the mythological and fabricated dimension of culture. It is not at all imperative that their gifts have to be known worldwide or their personhood removed from the ordinary ebb and flow of the local community. When giftedness stays "at home," when we realize how many gifted people God has actually created, and when we understand that there are innumerable people who are just as good as—sometimes better than—the famous, but because they are not famous they are not esteemed nearly as highly, it is not difficult to imagine how much richer both the local church and the school systems would be if more gifted people simply chose to stay at home. Every CCM artist has the power to decide whether to stay home or join the other dimension. If they choose to join it, it is especially imperative for those who lead a pluralistically rich and christianly integrative life to take time to write thoughtful articles for young people, to do more public speaking, and to do part-time college teaching or teaching regularly in Sunday school or youth groups—all as a part of a thoroughly articulated Christian world-view. We must be entirely fair here. Not every CCM artist is gifted in the areas of writing or teaching; unfair burdens should not be placed on them. But those who have these gifts should use them to the full, even if it means cutting back on their musical output.

The Ongoing Question of Quality

As has been suggested, CCM artists seem to prefer content with a wide variety of stylistic replications over innovation. This means that CCM artists must squarely face issues of quality. The first is the ever-present temptation to validate a body of music according to its effectiveness in ministry. This is as wrong for Christians as offering a blemished animal was for the Jews (Deuteronomy 15:21). Any concept of ministry that knowingly excludes quality runs contrary the Scriptures. From the design of the tabernacle to that of the temple—including information about the rigorous training of the temple musicians—through the apostle Paul's instructions concerning decency, order, and excellence, and clear on into the description of the new heavens and the new earth, there is no hint anywhere in the Scriptures that mediocrity is excused in the name of service and ministry.

The second issue around quality is the temptation to use technology to hide mediocrity and dilettantism. This action increases the error of spiritualizing mediocrity by lying about quality— making it appear to be there when it isn't. When musicians are talented, why is all this technology needed? These comments are not at all directed against technology but against its misuse and its power to cover up. We should be thankful for all the technology at our disposal as well as for the artists who use it wisely and creatively.

The third issue is the temptation to overproduce in order to stay in or keep near the top forty. As is so often the case, overproduction results in decreased quality. The Peter principle comes into play, and many artists soon rise to the level of their incompetence. While this can and does happen in any field of artistic creativity, it should be particularly avoided by Christians. Personal excellence is not driven by time, fame, or deadlines. For discerning Christian artists, this might mean finding a creative pace that matches their gifts. And this in turn might mean slowing down, even at the risk of dropping out of public sight.

CCM: In the World, of the World

Some CCM musicians, including those in jazz, are being criticized for "going secular" by choosing to perform in jazz and blues clubs and other "secular" places, by writing songs without specific Christians messages, or by performing established secular tunes, ballads, and lyrics. *This criticism is entirely unfair and biblically groundless.* It is an unfortunate continuation of the old sacred/secular dualism. There are two reasons to support CCM artists "going secular."

First, all truth is God's truth even when God or Christ or salvation are not particularly mentioned in wholesome lyrics. It makes every bit of sense for a Christian artist to sing of love, justice, friendship, family, parades, pain, hurt, abuse, playfulness, children, games, brotherly and sisterly love, and any number of other conditions, as long as they are driven by the same conscience and care that drive straight-ahead Christian lyrics. CCM artists know that when the music making is over, they are accountable—as all of us are—for the kind and amount of direct witness they do. They also know that artistic excellence is its own kind of witness.

Second, many CCM artists have come to realize that as long as they limit themselves to playing only in "Christian" contexts, CCM, instead of reaching non-Christians, repeats itself to Christians, for whom it is not much more than spiritualized background music—a kind of holy wallpaper decorating their days. So some artists have chosen to target the unchurched by going directly to them with good, clean, moralizing and civilizing, gospel-ready messages. And this is good.

However, there is a dramatic difference between doing secular things christianly and becoming secularized. We have already raised questions as to the extent that CCM artists may be subtly secularized by what they may do to satisfy the gatekeepers and how they may allow the fabrications, dislocations, and overt commercialism to dilute their worldview. There is a further issue having to do with the way CCM artists can confuse their respect for the talent *and technique* of non-Christian artists with the *content* of their work.

It doesn't take long to discover that a significant proportion of popular music and MTV combines questionable, if not objectionable, content and extremely sophisticated production techniques. While Christian artists have a responsibility to become as technically and artistically proficient as possible, they cannot afford to overlook or relativize content—theirs or anybody else's. When they do—and some have done it publicly and enthusiastically—they fail a primary tenet: In worded/deeded art forms, the morality of content is preeminent.

We can take this further. If content is subordinated to talent and production, then is CCM's Christian content all that important, or is it at the mercy of production—simply along for the ride? Is it just one of any number of content options, all of which are at the service of technique, image, and production? No Christian artist can make the mistake of implying that morally objectionable content and Christian content are implicitly on an equal footing *as long as there is a good show of talent, technique, and production*. If content is not all that important, then why all the fuss in the first place about Christians entering the pop market in order to specifically introduce Christian content into an otherwise satisfying context?

In sum, it is crucial to understand that if CCM artists are accused of overdoing things, it should be on the side of a carefully articulated Christian witness and Christian mindset. When we consider the enormous force and complexity in the secular marketplace: its gatekeeping and fabrications; mistaken concepts of locale and identity; production, technique, and image over substance; and when we consider the potential danger in the acquisition of status, power, and money, then we can understand the alternatives CCM faces: succumbing even more to its own secularization or becoming all the more Christian—purifying its witness so effectively that, in the spirit of Christ himself, it gives up certain prerogatives in order to reform where no one else dares. Anything less further confuses an already confused youth culture.

CCM and the American Character

On the positive side, Americans hear themselves variously described as inventive, outgoing, nationally generous and forgiving, tolerant, loving, idealistic, practical, and easygoing. On the negative side, they are said to be materialistic, hedonistic, selfish, crime-ridden and morally bankrupt, ecologically careless, self-indulgent, and greedy. And because of the moral, cultural, and behavioral diversity of America, both lists could arguably be said to pertain simultaneously, even paradoxically.

But two attributes, describing the very character of Christ, are seldom mentioned: meekness and lowliness of heart. What does it mean for an entire society to be meek and lowly of heart, or are these attributes privately reserved for individuals? This doesn't make sense because individual behavior can never be kept to itself. How individuals behave helps describe what the family is, and what the family is influences the next societal unit, and so on, until the broad character of cultures and nations discloses itself.

This being true, what about the arts? If meekness and lowliness of heart don't quite describe our broad cultural ways, what about popular Christian music? It is difficult to avoid the hype, the glitter, the opulence, and the swagger of much of it. The megabatteries of sound, the overkill of gesture and costume, the persistently loud, the driven, the commercially and editorially exaggerated, and the soloistic come to mind. Given the nature of the popular media, it is difficult to think of an overarching, broadly influential body of Christian music and musicians who have given themselves over to quieting the soul and giving rest to the spirit, especially to our children and young people. And it is equally difficult to find young people, aspiring to be the next Christian stars, who conceive of their future as local servants, apart from the world of tours, concerts, CD's, and a christianized version of fame. There are exceptions, but it is something near tragic that they remain exceptions or are perceived to be also-rans because they cannot quite make it past the gatekeepers to the top forty.

Put another way, if Christ were a musician instead of a carpenter, living in contemporary America, how would he make music? Would the industry allow him to show his meekness his way, or would a commercially palatable version of it be "suggested" from which he would have to turn away? And in doing so, would he reject the bigger-louder-more-is-better artistry that seems to characterize so much of what we regularly take in? Then how would he hold his audience? In all of this, we must understand that true meekness is really strength, boldness, tenderness, force, passion, and integrity, shown in servanthood and burden bearing. Meekness and lowliness are not the same as sonic shrivel or personal withdrawal, but complete qualities through which everything from joyous celebration to uncompromising protest, quiet nurturing, and redemptive grieving are expressed. All Christian musicians must examine themselves and their work to discover whether the magnification of gesture and image and the commercially exaggerated have drowned out the quiet, submissive, and broken spirit.

CCM: Shallow and Deep Content

These two issues are particularly pertinent to the subject of CCM.[5] Popular music, whether good or bad, is to a large extent shallow content. It does not call for deep intellectual or perceptual skills, otherwise it would not be popular. Even so, those who love popular music may often be deeply moved by its content. Assuming that we are talking about the best pop and the best CCM (including theologically sound lyrics), this is all right as far as it goes.

The problem is that with much of CCM this *is* as far as it goes. In CCM, production techniques and musical technique might be complicated, at times virtuosic, but they consistently feed into or ornament shallow content. But the gospel, the Christian life, the multiple issues in Christian living, the integration of faith and learning—these and more are both shallow *and* deep, milk *and* meat. When the ongoing perceptual mode and the ongoing accumulation of content are limited to the shallow, something is wrong with the way Christians go about the business of living christianly. While the makers of CCM cannot be entirely blamed for the perceptual shallowness of Christians, many of them should be faulted for giving the impression that this is all there is and for furnishing shallow musical and lyrical content.

While much of the same can be said for Christian classical music, there is a crucial difference. Christian classical is linked to a vast body of masterpieces, the total content of which challenges musical and spiritual perception to the very depths. And every Christian is personally responsible to go deep not only with the gospel but also with the artistic handiwork that parallels its depth. While we should never say that popular music is out of place in Christian expression, we must protest when shallowness is the chief preference. The gospel is heavy and it is deep. The question is: How can CCM point beyond shallowness toward deeper engagement with deepening content?

CCM, Corporate Song, and the Singing Voice

As with virtually all vocal pop music, CCM depends on strongly individualized styling. It is of the very nature of popular music that no two singers sound alike—the more differentiated the personal style, the better. It only follows that in a field as extensive as American popular music, we can hear vocal qualities that range from the guttural to the raucous to the mellow to the plaintive. In many cases, these stylings are developed at huge cost to the vocal instrument itself. Vocal health is far too often considered less important than simply getting a unique, differentiated sound.

While this problem is not new to popular vocal music, and while it is unwise to insist that classical singing styles should dominate popular music, the issue of vocal health has never been any more pressing than it is now, given the twin phenomena of vocal rock and electronic distortion/enhancement.

The issue of vocal health cannot be separated from the demise of curriculum-based musical training in the public schools. Children are no longer taught basic musicianship, nor are they introduced to the rudiments of individual and corporate singing as a regular part of their general education. The net effect is that America is losing its corporate singing voice and its sense of communal song. In its place is individualized, soloistic, and often distorted singing. And young people respond by wanting to be soloists.

The church has participated in this demise and has suffered because of it, despite the fact that corporate song is the heart of church music. It would be enough to say that the overwhelming influence of secular pop has caused this. But it doesn't stop there. CCM participates in the same message: individualized soloism is the center; corporate and choral song are secondary.

Thus as good as CCM may have become, it has done almost nothing to provide the church with models for corporate song. There is no encouragement whatsoever for simple, unadorned, choral song. Instead it's the solo; and these soloistic qualities, so naively imitated, are virtually useless when it comes to blending into an ensemble. And if this kind of singing includes vocal distortion, the problem is doubled: corporate singing is minimized and simple biblical principles regarding the care of our bodies are ignored.

The human voice is a delicate instrument. Before any singing style can be addressed or developed, singers must understand the nature of the instrument, how it functions, how it is to be kept healthy, and what its limitations are. Vocal imitation can create problems, especially if a young singer tries to mimic the sounds of another singer without knowing basic vocal technique. If the singer has a good ear, he or she may be able to imitate quite successfully, risking not only the loss of personal uniqueness but also damage to the voice. And once the damage is discovered it is often too late to repair it. By contrast, a healthy voice is free and capable of a wide range of pitches and individualized color. Good training and sensible vocal care need not inhibit the discovery of a unique sound. It simply guards against abuse in its development. No matter how tempting it is to go for a "different" sound, no Christian should give in to vocal abuse. No one has ever been called to glorify God by misusing God's handiwork.

There is one further implication of solo singing, this time a musical one. Many contemporary congregational songs are either direct takeovers of solos or freshly composed stylizations of them. In either case, they contain musical tasks that are inappropriate for amateur corporate singing: embellishments, drawn-out phrasings, and fluid shifts in rhythm. The result is a sloppy hybrid: congregations trying to sing solos, missing pitches, blurring ornamentations, muddling up syncopations, and generally ignoring the subtle interplay of pitch and text.

All of this brings us around to children. Given the weakened conditions of arts education in the public schools; given the soloistic slant of CCM and secular pop; and given the many media role models who abuse their voices, one of the few communities left to rescue these little ones is the church. By all accounts, the most important people in culture are teachers of children. It is crucial that the church undertake, as an integral part of its education program, the musical education of its children, especially with regard to singing. After all, the church is commanded, as a body, to sing. And commandments cannot be sloughed off simply because the church wants to do everything the way secular culture does it. And one of the things secular culture is doing is failing the children. While CCM shares in this issue, it should not bear the entire brunt. But along with the church, CCM must find a way of encouraging corporate song, of providing examples of simple, unforced singing. These efforts must first of all be for the children. It may be too late for the teenagers.

Perhaps the best way to summarize this entire section is to return to the concept of leadership. CCM artists have enormous influence. Many of them are artistically gifted and devout Christians. Their music making is better than it used to be, even though it has yet to transform the music of secular culture. These artists must face more squarely the world of secular music, its commercial driving forces, gatekeeping, fabrications, quantitative glut, affluence, and shallowness. They must come to understand more fully how one-sided their influence on young people is, how they have unwittingly given so much credence to soloism and have led so many people away from the more biblical concept of corporate song and local servanthood. All of these concerns can be summed up in this question: Given CCM's enormous influence, how can it turn its efforts and admirers toward more complete musical awareness, and how can it more prophetically lead the way in confronting and transforming the very world of which it has so much become a part?

What's Right with CCM?

How do we go about talking of the values of CCM after we have criticized both it and American culture? Isn't CCM somehow part of, even derived from, the larger world just described? And aren't there some things wrong with it that somehow affect what CCM is? While the answer to both questions may be yes, CCM is, in significant ways, different from the musical culture from which it takes its roots, partly because the very nature of music itself allows for it to break away from its original context.

CCM and a Pluralistic Musical Culture

CCM captures the spirit of a pluralistic musical culture; CCM likewise eases the relationship between sacred and secular popular music. Musically, CCM takes in every popular style from simple folk music to punk rock to rap to New Age; it uses certain kinds of jazz and even on occasion delves into semi- and pseudoclassical stylings. It is a compendium, musically speaking, of everything that popular culture is.

Textually, it is also a compendium of everything that popular theology is. While the general poetic or narrative styles of its lyrics are parallel to its secular counterparts, CCM's basic content is straight, clean, spiritual, moralizing, helpful, hopeful, generally redemptive, and, not infrequently, protesting. These messages get through, whatever the artistic quality or biblical compactness of the lyrics might be.

As to its general physical, gestural, and multimedia components, CCM once again takes its general cues from its secular counterparts. There is something for nearly everybody—a Christian counterpart to whatever the secular choices might be: everything from megaproductions to quiet, intimate, deeply personalized offerings. The real break away from the secular—and it is truly significant—lies in CCM's consistent avoidance of anything overtly sexual, anything verbally or gesturally off-color, or anything smacking of violence and aberration. This does not mean that there is no crudeness or cheapness, for a good part of popular culture is crude, rough-edged, raucous, overly loud, tattered, and unkempt. But we must keep in mind that crudeness can be a style, within which both moral and immoral actions may take place. And the very avoidance of sexual, abusive, and violent content in CCM, *even though its musical content may be similar to the secular counterparts that contain these*, is a strong testimony to those who continually find fault with it. Suffice it to say, there are countless CCM musicians and music lovers who are to be trusted when they say that their music making—whatever its style and aesthetic quality—is an act of love and a sacrifice of praise.

Improved Quality

CCM is better now than it used to be. There was a time when CCM struggled for any kind of respect. A lot of it represented a classic example of sincere Christians not only imitating, but imitating badly. But things are different of late. Christian pop is now out of the closet, freely at work among its secular counterparts. There is some very good music being made, and the general world of popular music recognizes this. CCM artists win Grammys; certain Christian artists have crossed over from being heard exclusively on Christian radio and television (this is more true of radio—Christian music on Christian television remains at a lower quality) to being seen and heard on network and cable media. This move toward excelling cannot be denied, even by CCM's harshest critics—some of whom are CCM musicians themselves—who tire of the trivia and mediocrity that still linger around them. It might even be said that CCM has done more to improve itself than the everyday classical music of the church—the ground-out anthems, the typical piano/organ arrangements, and the handbell music. Not a little of these are locked up in cliché, formula, and atrophied classicism—not-so-good wine in old wineskins.

CCM and Spiritual Integrity

Many CCM artists are not only musically gifted, they possess deep personal and spiritual integrity. In short, they love the Lord Jesus, they maintain a close personal walk with him, and they take advantage of every opportunity to make this known. This is true in spite of all the hype that superstardom has brought to CCM, and it remains true in spite of all the ways in which countless CCM groupies idolize the artists and miss the deeper artistic and spiritual point of what they are trying to do. While the question must eventually be raised as to why CCM has allowed itself to buy into the big-time superstar mentality of American culture, there can be no doubt that when all the publicity, hype, and megasize of the best of CCM is stripped away, there remains a nucleus of artistic and spiritual integrity that should earn the respect of every musical pluralist.

This nucleus of integrity often spells the difference between those who seek fame without paying attention to excellence and servant-hood and those to whom fame comes without compromising either the quest for excellence or spiritual integrity. Lamentably, few young people who want to be the next Michael Card or Phil Keaggy understand how technically demanding and individually styled this kind of music is and how unqualified they are to carry it out to the full. They overlook quality and discipline in the name of ministry, naively assuming that music ministers simply because it is Christian and that they too can minister simply because they are Christian. In the meantime, they may skip right over quality, creativity of content, and discipline. And it is also this very error that has crept into the work of some of the better-known CCM musicians. They too have come to excuse a lapse in quality, perhaps because what they are doing still seems to "minister" and because they remain Christians. Meanwhile, this frustrates and embarrasses the better CCM musicians.

CCM as an Alternative

CCM offers young people solid and useful alternatives to its secular counterparts. In other words, it fights and joins at the same time. Whatever is "out there" stylistically in secular pop, CCM offers a response on the same musical terms. Even though the personal styles of certain secular artists are beyond imitation, there is enough variety and creativity in CCM to challenge the majority of younger Christians. Meanwhile, CCM can make an even more powerful impact on the young in direct proportion to the manner in which the truly gifted stars maintain their uniqueness, whatever the cost.

Once again, it must be said that in a field as variegated and stylistically proliferated and competitive as pop and rock are, ministry alone won't cut it. Excellence and uniqueness—two normal qualities for radically gifted and reborn people—must be relentlessly pursued. To the extent that they are, CCM will be all the more effective as an alternative to what the secular world offers. This could mean that CCM's ranks should shrink; CCM could well become less popular; and a significant number of its artistic dwarfs should fall by the wayside. So be it, as long as the cause of Christ is all the more effectively served. Christian musicians must continually remember that size and prestige all by themselves are not an effective alternative to secularism. In fact, they may play into its very hands.

CCM and Ministry

CCM ministers. Despite the criticisms levelled at those who use the grand biblical word *ministry* to justify virtually everything, it remains true that for the Christian, music and ministry cannot be separated. In the most fundamental sense, a ministry is a nurturing, building, or healing action undertaken by at least one person, by faith and in Christ's name, for at least one other person. A ministry is not determined by size, quantity, scope, familiarity, popularity, strangeness, or medium. It is simply the power of God being made perfect in the weakness of someone for the benefit of another. All musicians who understand this, employing all kinds of music, making music everywhere—in concert halls, homes, churches, coffeehouses, nursing homes, hospices, prisons, nurseries, and opera house—are ministers of music.

It is to this extent alone that CCM ministers. This is different from saying that CCM *alone* ministers. It has no special ministry because it is CCM, because it is popular, or because it is overwhelmingly everywhere, but because God has decided to work in the midst of its making. Thus God is the author and finisher of all ministries, while the ministers themselves, along with the particular media they employ, are simply willing, unworthy, and surrendered servants.

While there are false concepts of ministry and false ministry itself—and no one knows this better than all truly discerning musicians—no one can deny that CCM can and does truly minister. CCM builds. CCM edifies; it heals; it unites; it binds up and soothes. There are far too many witnesses to these graces for anyone to deny them. What remains for the entire church, not just the music makers, is to rediscover a true theology of ministry. As that is undertaken, CCM will not disappear from the ministerial map. In fact, rediscovery could well assist in its continuing reform.

NOTES

1. Quentin J. Schultze, et al., *Dancing in the Dark* (Grand Rapids: Eerdmans, 1991), p. 51. This is a significant work. It should be read by every thinking Christian. It is temperate and evenhanded, though not without its indictments. Documentation is thorough (the extensive bibliography is worth the price of the book), the writing style is clear and consistent, and the insights are carefully structured and penetrating. While the authors write from a Christian point of view, they seem to be especially careful to avoid the trap of superficial moralizing and alarmist theology. This may disappoint some readers who may be looking for lists of dos, don'ts, rights, wrongs, and slogans. Unlike some Christian writings on popular culture, which mimic writing and thinking styles derived out of the very culture being criticized, *Dancing in the Dark* stands out as a noteworthy approach to an enormously complex scene. Interestingly enough, *Dancing in the Dark* does not take up the subject of CCM. One can only guess that the authors wanted the readers to focus on the larger picture and to infer that CCM could not exist in its present state without the prior influences of secular pop, just because it is Christian.

2. Schultze, et al., *Dancing in the Dark*, pp. 131ff.

3. Schultze, et al., *Dancing in the Dark*, p. 132.

4. Schultze, et al., *Dancing in the Dark*, pp. 59–60.

5. Chapter 6, pp. 124–125, 133–135.

Chapter 9

THE PRACTICE OF CHURCH MUSIC (I): MUSIC AND THE WORSHIPING CHURCH

The Lord God has spoken! Who can but prophesy?

—AMOS 3:8b (NASB)

It is not enough that a thing be beautiful; it must be suitable to the subject, and there must be in it nothing of excess or defect.

—PASCAL, *Pensees*

Church Music and the Scriptures

The Scriptures deal with church music two ways, through narrative and principle. Each has particular importance. The narrative portions, beginning in Genesis with the mention of Jubal the prototypical music maker, and going through numerous accounts of musical usage in everyday life—from weddings to wars—in the temple, religious festivals, and the early Church show us that music making was for everybody in every place and that all practitional bases were covered a long time ago. In other words, the task of the contemporary church is not to think up new combinations of music and circumstance—for there are none—but to be sure that its actions are creative and appropriate.

As important as it is to know about these different practices, it is just as important to understand that no particular practice or set of practices is said to be more important or meritorious than another. Some people have decided that Old Testament temple worship is the ideal and have built huge musical edifices to prove it. Sometimes these have succeeded, as in best classical church traditions. At other times they turn into parodies, often in our contemporary American megachurches, where size and quality often get out of balance with each other. Other people believe that New Testament practices are the only ones to follow. And since instrumental music is not specifically mentioned, musical instruments are not permitted. In other worshiping communities, only the singing of psalms or metrical versions of them is allowed. Some churches prohibit the use of professional musicians or disallow any music making except congregational song.

Even though some might disagree with these limitations, everyone must acknowledge that wonderful music has grown up in the midst of each. There is a lesson in this: Honorable people, following their convictions as to what the Scriptures actually allow and making music out of their conscience-informed creativity, will never want for quality or authenticity, simply for having limited themselves. One could wish that more churches would ask themselves these three simple questions before they create musical programs: How much and what kind(s) of music do we need? How much and what kind(s) do we simply want? By what biblical and theological principles do we make our choices?

This brings us to the second way the Scriptures deal with music making, through disclosing principles. We are going to take the position that what we find in the Old Testament is just as important as what we find in the New. To put it another way, there is no musical equivalent in the New Testament to Jesus' words: "This is what Moses said, but I say to you. . . ." We can therefore safely assume that the limited writings in the New Testament about music stand as further comment on the Old Testament and not as any sort of replacement. Thus the whole counsel of God regarding musical practice can flow out of a whole view of the Bible.

These music-making principles can be reduced to five. They are simple and comprehensive, as all principles should be. And just as it has been impossible to keep the subject of music making in the church out of the general discussion, it is just as impossible to assume that the following principles apply just to those who make music in the church.

1. *Singing is not an option; it is a commandment.* "Sing to the Lord a new song" (Psalm 96:1). This commandment is not reserved just for professional musicians; it is for everybody everywhere. The principal direction of all singing is to the Lord. Singing is an act, and for all Christians, it can only be an act of worship. Although this passage suggests that new songs take priority, old songs sung newly are just as important as songs done for the first time.

2. *Playing instruments to the Lord is just as forcefully commanded as singing.* This can be seen particularly in Psalms 147, 149, and 150. Some object to instrumental music either because it is not mentioned specifically in the apostle Paul's instructions to the church or because instrumental music does not carry texted messages. While both these things are true, the psalms make it very clear that we must speak up on instruments even though we cannot speak truth with them. But by being commanded, it is very evident that, in God's view, this kind of speaking up is necessary or it would not have been commanded in the first place. Furthermore, this commandment, by extension, authorizes the presence of other nonverbal forms of worship: gestures, artifacts, architectures, fragrances, and the like. The only possible error in introducing these into worship is one of assuming that they can equal, become more important than, or preempt the verbal.

3. *In texted music, there is a distinction between the role of the text and that of music.* We find this in a key passage contained in Paul's instructions in Ephesians 5:19: "Speaking to one another in psalms and hymns and spiritual songs, singing and making melody with your heart to the Lord" (NASB). Paul first recognizes the didactic importance of these song types *as text*, therefore as proclamation and teaching (speak to another). He then shifts the direction by instructing the Christians to make music, or as some translations put it, to make melody, in (with) their hearts *to the Lord.*

Two things are clarified in this distinction. Following on Psalm 96:1, music is made first of all to the Lord and only secondarily to each other. Music is incapable of teaching what only truth can teach. At the same time we instruct one another with text, we are making music to the Lord as a corporate body.

4. *The integration of mind and spirit makes for the best music.* This principle also comes from Paul's teachings. It is found in his discussion of prophecy and tongues (1 Corinthians 14). In verse 14, he maintains that when one prays in tongues, one's spirit prays while one's mind remains unfruitful. He then goes on to suggest that there is a kind of praying in which spirit and mind work together. He than couples this kind of praying to a certain kind of singing, again in which mind and spirit are integrated.

From this, we can gather that music making that comes about in the midst of frenzy or ecstasy or any situation in which "spirit" is preeminent is not fully valuable until the mind is equally involved. Paul is not suggesting that such music making is wrong any more than tongues are wrong. Rather, he is speaking about the preferred and most effective ways of conducting oneself in public worship. This principle reaches directly into the classic tension between the Dionysian and Apollonian, the debates about romanticism and classicism, intuition and cognition. Paul is saying that in matters of mind and spirit, balance is better than extremism.

5. *When all Scripture references to music making are combined, we learn that we are to make music in every conceivable condition: joy, triumph, imprisonment, solitude, grief, peace, war, sickness, merriment, abundance, and deprivation.* This principle implies that the music of the church should be a complete music, not one-sided or single faceted. And in the spirit of Paul's instructions about praying (Philippians 4:6), we should make music in the same way, with thanksgiving, whatever our condition.

Not All Churches Can Be Artistic Leaders

The church is not, at base, an artistic enterprise. It is not a professional arts organization. It is, in a very wonderful sense, a crazy-quilt gathering of all kinds of people from all walks of life and all levels of intelligence, intellect, and artistic sensitivity. There are small churches, large churches, poor churches, rich churches, and everything in between. Some churches can muster up a choir of no more than eight or nine singers, mostly sopranos and altos and one baritone. They have no money for music or fine instruments. They sing in and out of tune without any kind of capable leadership. Musical choices, by even the most tolerant standards, may be poor. Yet they are doing the very best they can, and, in fact, they are doing better than they did a month ago, because a new family joined the church last week and the husband is A TENOR. *And yet, that church is just as responsible as the most artistically affluent churches to preach a gospel crammed to the full with sound doctrine, including wise and insightful counsel on worship, artistic creativity, excellence, and radical newness.*

When it comes right down to it, very few churches can programmatically fulfill the mandates of the very theology of the arts they must preach. *There is a distinct difference between the church providing a radically correct theological base for the best art done in the best way in a context of newness, and the church being responsible for doing this Sunday by Sunday, parish by parish.* The failure to discern this has led many churches into a feeling of inferiority, others into an overprogrammed display of pseudonewness, and still others into a life of aesthetic idolatry. The more pressing artistic task of the church is to ensure that even if it honestly cannot lead culture musically from within, it can preach a theology of artistic action and response, which is leaderly, freeing all artists to create freely and newly and equipping all receivers of art to respond in the same spirit. In this way, the church with one tenor and the church with the limitless resources will have the same mind, the same message, and the same integrity.

Worship and Musical Appropriateness

Two questions confront everyone who wants to evaluate music wisely. The first is the qualitative one, addressed in chapters 4 and 6: What is good music? The second is one of context and function: What (good) music is good for what?

The relationship between content and context is one of the great issues in musical practice. It ranges all the way from the seemingly innocent question of choosing just the right music for a quiet dinner party to choices that reach directly into the issue of musical relativity and moral absolutes, as we saw in chapter 2. And there is probably no cross-section of human experience to which this issue more seriously applies than to the musical choices of the worshiping church.

The main reason why musical appropriateness is such a weighty subject for the church is because the subject cannot be disconnected from central matters of faith and practice. The consequences of music making, therefore of choice and appropriateness, have eternal value. Everything done musically must be defended or critiqued theologically and biblically. Church music does not exist for its own sake; nor is it, as some would have it, just a tool. Nor is it part of a setup—half behavioral and half spiritual—for the allegedly more important activities of worship. Music is, in its own way, proclamation and as such is completely accountable. Musical appropriateness, therefore, is more than stylistic conjunction (or disjunction) or some sort of aesthetic politeness and propriety. It is first of all an issue of faith musically put to work, shown through discerning choice.

Following hard after this, musical appropriateness is never a matter of pragmatics but rather of wisdom. It is not a question of what works or gets a certain job done; this simply puts music back into the role of behavioral agent. Rather, it is a question of what is best for the worshiping community at the time. The union of music and function, as we have seen, can be traced all the way back into God's way of putting the creation together: everything that God makes has worth and everything that has worth functions. Putting it this way unites musical action with function with purpose. *Thus it is proper to say that all musical choices should be purposefully and functionally appropriate, with excellence continually assumed.*

If quality has a thousand tongues, it should not be difficult—in fact, it should be downright enjoyable—for Christian music makers to match musical style, type, length, difficulty, simplicity, and complexity with whatever else is taking place. Error creeps in when music for music's sake, or music for results' sake, intrudes into, limits, or compromises the choosing.

The error of music for results' sake can creep in, in the name of musical pluralism when "becoming all things to all people" invites a sloppy, indiscriminate musical hash in the name of variety, creativity, and ecclesiastical multiculturalism. In these contexts everything is appropriate because, in some way, everyone has to be reached. Church music then turns out to be something like a closeout sale—something for everybody at reduced cost. While the question of quality may be blatantly disregarded, the deeper problem lies in the complete absence of authenticity.

This brings us back to the importance of centeredness in any pluralistic effort. Churches that try to offer an indiscriminate assortment of musics, to cover all the bases, overlook the more central fact of uniqueness. Uniqueness never comes about just by presenting assortments. If it did, the dictionary would be the ideal piece of literature, simply because it has the most comprehensive assortment of words imaginable. "Something for everybody" does not make for good church life, even though it might make for good advertising. But advertising does not concern itself with telling people what to buy as dictated by their needs. It manipulates them into creating needs out of wants and assuming that wanting and needing are really the same thing.

For advertising, this is appropriate. But not for the church. The gospel dictates a different kind of appropriateness. It is centered squarely in the conviction that people need something whether they want it or not. This means that, in a quite radical way, the church is a prescriptive organism, ready to go to the point of death, deprivation, and even shrinkage in order to keep the prerogatives of the cross in focus. "All things to all people," in the larger theological context in which the apostle Paul was thinking, was never meant to be interpreted the way many people interpret it. To "become like" does not mean to imitate or provide an equivalent. It means to understand any contrary worldview or any fraction of it in order to know what to do about it, rather than simply to describe and accommodate it. Then the gospel provides the answer, the right-side-up answer, with such force and straightforwardness that people are brought to startling conclusions about God, sin, and salvation.

Church music must follow suit. Indiscriminate musical choice for the sake of attracting everybody means that there is no real centeredness, no practitional authenticity. At first blush, this sounds like a refutation of everything said and defended so far about pluralism. It is not. It is, however, a refutation of *faceless* pluralism, given these facts: (1) the best pluralists will always have limited, not infinite, choice; (2) pluralism never substitutes for the pursuit of excellence; (3) pluralism is the act of discovering and relating to the centeredness of others from the vantage point of one's own centeredness.

This last point is especially crucial. If, from my centeredness, I reach out to the centeredness of others, I will have never lost my identity, even though I am reaching out. On the other hand, if I reach out to the centeredness of others without my knowing who I am, *they may well assume that my reaching out is a sign that I want to become like them.* Therefore, there is every reason to believe that indiscriminate musical choice, while attracting great numbers of people, may well send out the wrong signals about the nature of the uniqueness of the gospel. As has been argued in several places, there is no intrinsic equation between musical content and worldview, but how well is this understood by those whose worldview is committed to worshiping creature instead of Creator? Musical appropriateness, in any church, is not properly discovered until these issues are considered fully.

While appropriateness and pluralism are by no means mutually exclusive, they must be kept in delicate balance. And there is every reason to assume that church x and church y may choose different music programs even though they are preaching the same gospel. What they cannot afford to do is to clone each other in order to keep up with each other, vying for souls. Rather, church x, out of Spirit-driven conscience, chooses a certain musical profile, a certain combination of centeredness and diversity. Church y goes another way with the same integrity. Meanwhile, the Holy Spirit works in any way, any place, or any time, irrespective of the merits, size, scope, or cost of one program over the other. While church y stays small and church x grows; while on the surface it might be tempting for y to copy x; while the praying and witnessing people go about their daily round of worship and outreach; while all these things go on, the Kingdom is built.

Each church has an obligation to discover for itself what appropriateness and authenticity are, realizing that it is but one carefully pruned and tended vine in the larger vineyard, depending upon God alone to determine its size. In the meantime, each church must realize that some people will be attracted to one musical program and not another. This being so, and each church deciding what it must be, the thing that will eventually hold the people or, in some mysterious way, turn them away is the integrity and authenticity of what is done. These will win over faceless variety and undisciplined entrepreneurialism.

Appropriateness, Familiarity, and Newness

Three positions can be taken with regard to the relationship of newness and familiarity to appropriateness. The first two represent the extremes:

1. The only appropriate music for worship is familiar music, not because the church should shun newness, but because continuity and flow within worship demand it.
2. The only appropriate music for the church is unfamiliar music, not because familiarity is bad, but because the new birth is the context for a new way and a new way demands new tongues, even in the contexts of corporate worship.
3. Both familiar and unfamiliar music are appropriate as long as the model for the use of each is sound, both theologically and practitionally.

While there is certain merit in the first two positions, we shall proceed through a number of steps to argue for the third.

Church music, in all of its types, styles, and media can only be made two main ways.

There is music that is made by some and heard by others. This type can take two forms: (1) The makers and the hearers maintain the same role throughout. This music includes virtually all anthems, vocal solos, and instrumental music. (2) The makers and hearers exchange roles. This music comprises responsorial music.

There is music that is made and heard by everybody at the same time. Corporate singing and hymnody in all of its forms, types, and presentational modes comprise this body. This is the heart of all church music, therefore the most important. Congregational song is not only primary because it is corporate. Of equal importance, in the union of text and music, is that the entire worshiping body is given full responsibility for singing to and about God and proclaiming the gospel. This further implies—and the rich history of hymnody has proven it possible—that the body of hymnody employed by any church is incomplete until, by constant use, it discloses the entire counsel of God. In other words, a congregation is just as responsible to sing the gospel as the preachers are to preach it. These two tasks (singing and preaching) jointly undertaken to their fullest, then reduce themselves to one common act: The church, through its joint priesthood of believers and ministers, is united in proclamation, and when undertaken in the power of God, there is no escaping the force of the proclamation. The whole world cannot help but hear.

One matter needs to be reintroduced before we can apply these ideas fully. In chapter 7, we took up the subject of faith and musical action. One of the points made was that faith, the fullest kind of faith, makes the familiar strange and the strange familiar. While this concept would appear to justify a random mix in worship, we need to be more careful than that. Each has its particular place, as follows.

1. *The familiar is the appropriate, therefore the preferred, mode in those parts of the worship where the ministering musicians and the*

congregation are musically at work together or in response to each other.

This includes all sung portions of the liturgy, including the hymnic singing within it, and any instrumental portions that either introduce, responsively follow, or summarize whatever is sung. A freely flowing liturgy, in any setting, whatever the musical style or sociomusical expectations of the worshipers, should be of one cloth. When it becomes a potpourri, an idiomatic free-for-all, a concoction brought about by musicians who confuse creativity with disorientation, the flow disappears and people get confused. Then when the time comes for genuine experiment and spontaneity, there is not much heart for undertaking them.

Not that these functional musics should remain static and unchanging. Change should come about, for change within function is appropriate. But it should be of the gradual kind. It should take its cues from the concepts of nearby pluralism, *as these are perceived by the worshiping laity to be nearby.* There is absolutely nothing wrong with the ministering musicians adjusting musical choice to the musical perceptions of the congregation in the functional parts of the liturgy. This is not aesthetic compromise but good sense. The musicians, then, must be capable of finding the excelling musics that meet the congregation's needs. And faith can be at work all along, because its role in the presence of familiarity or any gradual move away from it is to ensure that all of these musickings remain new—sung as if for the first time. The danger in perpetually linking repeated music to worship is that it becomes the expected. The expected then becomes the addictive, and worship turns into conditioned reflex, the exact opposite of faithful action. Any clever church musician knows that the best way to induce worshipers into "sensing the presence of God" is to misuse familiar and repeated music. The music then acts upon the worshiper instead of the worship acting with the music. As stated elsewhere, this might well be idolatry.

This equation of repetition with God's presence represents one of the most puzzling things about some kinds of charismatic worship and praise services, which may not be as spontaneous and free as claimed. In these settings, certain songs seem always to prompt the raising of hands or standing up, while others do not. Other songs are used in nearly changeless combination, as if they were designed to achieve a certain climax, effect, or behavior. Discerning worship leaders must sense that when familiarity begins to turn into conditioned reflex or the right worship atmosphere cannot be achieved unless certain music is used, they are responsible to correct the worshipers and lead them back into the way of faith.

2. *The new and strange are the appropriate modes in those worship contexts where music is done by some and heard by others (anthems and instrumental music), and in the extraliturgical music making of the church, where special concerts, recitals, and festivals are offered by the church both for its own enrichment as well as for the general public.*

In both contexts, but especially the first, care must be taken to introduce new and different music in carefully discerned quantities and increments. In both contexts, the burden is placed upon the faithful willingness of the congregation to engage in newness and to demonstrate to itself and to the world that truth and gospel make new creatures in Christ and that these new creatures make, receive, and hilariously offer new creations.

Perhaps the best way to summarize this entire section is to provide an analogy. Music that is appropriately familiar could be called *diaconal*. It supports, lays on hands, ministers, serves, provides, nurtures, bears burdens, gives solace, and heals. When newness is appropriate, music takes on the role of the *prophetic* and *oracular*. This is the music of change, reform, disturbance, sojourn, challenge, upheaval, and breaking away. The two together, the diaconal and the prophetic, constitute a ministry of music that is complete and, in its completeness, appropriate.

Church Music: Sound and Silence

There is such a thing as too much music, even when all the music is good music, in the same sense that there is such a thing as too much food even when all of it is nutritious. Musical gluttony is not uncommon either in general culture or in Christian music making. In fact, it is virtually beyond argument that music is so nearly omnipresent in our lives that it has become absent, not in the acoustical sense, but in the sense of having true significance.[1] If we were to keep a tally of all the times we hear music during the day—in stores, at work, in our automobiles, on television, radio, and stereo sets, day in and day out—the total would be overwhelming. Then, if we were to do a set of comparisons: (1) between the amount of music that reaches our ears and the amount of music we consciously perceive; (2) between the amount of music that serves as background and the amount that functions in direct connection with another activity—for there is a distinct difference; and (3) between the amount of music heard or listened to in all of the above circumstances and the amount we actually sit down and listen to just for the challenge and joy of perceiving music for what it inherently is, we would probably discover that the first situation in each comparison would win out. In other words, despite the overwhelming presence of music in our lives, very little of it has any direct significance.

This has carried over into our perception and use of music in worship. We would be better off if we forced ourselves into musical silence in order to discover two things: (1) that it is quite possible to worship God without music; God will still keep company with us in our silence; and (2) that music making is at its best, not when we engorge ourselves with it, but when, as lean and spare worshipers—temperate and spiritually fit in all things—we make music in exactly the right amount.

Part of the sound-silence problem is the result of tradition, part is caused by our culturewide obsession with busyness, and part by a misconception of the deeper meaning of community.

1. *Sound, silence, and tradition.* In the previous section we spoke of the two main ways that all church music is done. Here we will refer to the first of these, namely when music is made by some and heard by others: anthems, solos, and instrumental music. It is this

music that has grown up into an almost independent body of practice within the larger contexts of corporate worship; it is this body of music that takes the most accurate theologizing to justify; and it is also this body of music that can so easily turn into a kind of concert-within-worship music.

In the earliest church music practices, this kind of music was either minimal or nonexistent. When it did occur it was responsorial in nature: there was singing or chanting and occasional instrumental response. As practices multiplied, as traditions began to evolve, and as specially trained singers and instrumentalists undertook more exclusive roles in the liturgy, the musical actions of the congregation (the laity) became more and more separated from those of the trained musicians. This separation not only took its initiative from the growing professionalization of church musicians, but from the larger tendency of the church to exclude the congregation from real, functional participation in any of the liturgy, let alone music.

Since the Reformation, Protestant church music, even in the smallest churches, has evolved toward increasing the role of musical specialists and musical specialties within corporate worship, *without specifically disengaging the congregation from its musical role.* This evolution is just as complex as the pre-Reformational one, perhaps even more, because of the pluralistic and decentralized nature of Protestantism itself. But while many good things have come of it, some problems remain, one of which is specifically related to the sound-silence question.

While instrumental music, as an independent musical action, is both justifiable and commanded, it is no more central to church music than solos or anthems are. Because congregational song is the central musical action of the church, the main function of instruments in congregational song is to introduce and support the singing. But we must remember that it is the very importance of congregational song that justifies the instrumental introductions and responses.

And this is why we now have what we call choral preludes or hymn preludes and arrangements. These evolved from the humble function of giving worshipers an idea of what melody to sing. As time passed and instrumentalists and congregations became more adept at what they were doing, these functional introductions took on an independence and sophistication of their own, to the point where the choral or hymn prelude was transformed into a sophisticated body of independent music. The evolution of this genre, coupled to a gradually evolving fancy for preludic, interludic, and postludic music, brings us to the problem: *How much of this pre-, inter-, and postludic music is appropriate, in that much of it takes place within a mixture of sound (usually talk) and silence (called for but not commonly observed, or called for and then backgrounded with music)?*

There are three possible solutions. First, preludes, interludes, and postludes could be included as a direct and organic part of worship, in which case they are to be co-offered in silence by the congregation. This would mean that the congregation would have to learn that the time of silence is not simple courtesy (although one could argue for silence in corporate worship for that reason alone), but a time when the worship of God demands listening as an offering.

Second, preludes and postludes could be done away with completely. In their place, conversation would be encouraged: the how-do-you-dos and good-byes, general socialization, small talk, and the like. In the meantime, instrumental music would be returned to its historical function of introducing, accompanying, or serving independently of choral and congregational song. The advantage of this approach is that it treats small talk honestly, and the musicians no longer need feel that their music is a cross between a doormat and an act of worship.

The third solution is probably the trickiest, in that it appears to be similar to the current mixture of music and talk found in so many churches. It is based on a very old idea that music and social interaction indeed can coexist very well, *as long as there is a prior understanding that this is supposed to be what happens*. The idea of listening to music in absolute silence is a good one, in that it provides a context for absolute concentration on the music—if desired—or thinking about other things while the music goes on. However, if by common agreement among musicians, pastoral leadership, and congregation, music and conversation are seen to be compatible *for some occasions in worship but not for others*, then music and talk can be legitimately and honestly integrated. Once again, this makes everything honest.

2. *Sound, silence, and contemporary culture.* We live in a busy, noisy, and socially uneasy culture. As culture has overprogrammed and overbusied itself, so has the church. Many worship leaders and committees see to it that every moment of time is filled with some activity—a kind of liturgical ant farm. The resurgence of interest in liturgics among evangelicals has promoted a flurry of ceremonial, gestural, verbal, and musical additives. The trouble with these is not in their inherent worth, but in the very fact that they are added. While many evangelicals concern themselves with liturgical activity they have yet to understand the deeper implications of liturgical worship, three of which apply to the sound-silence problem.

A *true liturgy, while possibly complicated, is not busy.* Nor is its complexity subject to whimsical experiment and pseudocreativity. The underlying structures and rhythms are such that experiment for experiment's sake fails. Yet those who understand the fundamental stability and richness of liturgy likewise understand how open it is to substantive creativity. While change and complexity may be present, there is never the flurry and self-conscious rush that mark the fabrications some contemporary churches seem so obsessed with.

A *true liturgy honors silence as more than a social amenity.* Silence is one of its many languages. Our overly busied congregations should seek out silence without feeling obligated to cover or background it with music. These cover-ups comprise the world of the musical interlude, the acoustical shelter for liturgical "dead space," created to help the silence out, to assist in handling this dread thing.

Silence is a natural part of a genuine community. Anybody who has ever attended a party or any kind of small social gathering has experienced the discomfort that comes when things suddenly go silent. Everybody gets nervous and scratches around for something to say, something to break this vacuous curse. Whatever is said, no matter its inanity or irrelevance, comes as a great relief. Someone has rescued the gathering from terminal embarrassment.

This silence happens when people don't know each other well or when they fail to understand the deeper significance of how well they actually *do* know each other, because certain social veneers have intervened. The more intimately people know each other, the more they are knit by deep relationships, and the more they genuinely love and trust each other, the longer they can enjoy silence—long periods of it—in each other's presence. In these contexts, silence is a healing and strengthening communion, a way of relating, a profoundly satisfying language. It is the furthest thing away from boredom or embarrassment.

The family of God is, or should be, bonded together in this way. Of all people on earth, with the possible exception of wife and husband, the church knows a corporate bonding that has its roots in none other that the person of Jesus Christ, made real by the action of Holy Spirit. The Apostles' Creed has it right when it speaks of the communion of the saints. When rightly understood and lovingly practiced, it provides the way for the kind of silence that only friends of the Savior can experience with each other. And the body of Christ worships peaceably and comfortably.

A Word About Hymns and Hymnbooks

Presently, the church is caught somewhere between its enormously rich musical heritage and an unprecedented rush of musical options and technologies. No one needs to be told this, nor do all the available options need to be described. The obsession with relevance and contemporaneity, the acceleration of style changes, the generally populist ethos, and the urge among evangelicals to spread the gospel as quickly and directly as possible, coupled to a general antipathy toward anything old, acoustic, or classical, have combined to make hymnbooks, hymn singing, and pipe organs the chief symbols of archaism. To many they are obsolete.

While there is nothing inherently wrong with change, there is something wrong with the wholesale rejection of tradition. Christianity is not just new, it is for all time. Christianity is not just contemporary language, it is classic language, time-honored and time-polished expression. Christianity is not just quick news, it is hard news, it is historically validated news, and it is longterm news.

Probably the most tragic and ironic aspect of the weeding out and displacement that so much of contemporary Christianity has undertaken is that the alleged newness is not all that new, because so much of it is borrowed. This simply means that the "contemporary" church is already behind, and as it tries to keep up with rapid change it will probably fall further behind. In addition, the very pluralism that the church attempts to espouse is contradicted by the exclusion of tradition and classical culture. Pluralism is not just choosing among present practices; pluralism should reach back and look ahead. The obsession with the immediately relevant precludes both, and it can be argued that losing a sense of history is a sign that there is no true vision for the future, just a repetition of the present.

Hymnbooks and hymn singing are not only important because they link us to the past; they contain some of the most tightly packed, concise doctrinal and devotional thought available. Furthermore, there is a renaissance of theologically rich hymn writing, of which the church should be taking greater notice. To the rich heritage of Watts, the Wesleys, Luther, Cowper, Montgomery, and Havergal, we can add the names of these outstanding contemporaries: Bishop Timothy Dudley-Smith, Fred Pratt Green, Fred Kaan, Bryan Jeffrey Leach, and Margaret Clarkson. They are not displacing the best of older hymnody, they have grown up in it, are adding to it, and are actively defending it. They cannot be neglected.

There is another reason why hymnbooks are important. They make us read. And we need to keep reading, both words *and* music. As important as oral tradition is, we also urgently need to keep alive the craft of reading music. Our young people have not been well nurtured in musical literacy. Reading music, especially for purposes of singing, is not encouraged, nor is it systematically taught. Given this condition, the church may well be the last place left for a carefully mounted program of training in musical literacy, especially singing. This does not just mean choral training, but singing and hymnic training as an integral part of Christian education. The rationale is simple. If the faith is truly to be learned, it must be taught. If singing the faith is crucial (and we know it is), then it too must be taught. The best way to do this is to combine the teaching and reading of Christian thought with the reading and singing of Christian hymnody, beginning as early as possible in a child's Christian education. Vigorous and informed singing is not simply frill. It is a fundamental way of rejoicing, praying, learning, worshiping, and proclaiming the gospel.

NOTES

1. See pages 134ff. for further elaboration.

Chapter 10

THE PRACTICE OF CHURCH MUSIC (II): MUSIC AND THE WITNESSING CHURCH

Everywhere I send you, you shall go, And all that I command you, you shall speak. Do not be afraid of them. . . .
—JEREMIAH 1:7b–8a (NASB)

Go, tell it on the mountain, over the hills and everywhere. . . .
—JOHN W. WORK

Witness is not the "other thing" that the worshiping church does. Musically speaking, it is not the downside of the real stuff: the art music, the formal, tried, true, and stable. Witnessing is not just something that specialists do while the rest of the church looks and prays on. And it is not that occasional contrived wedging of Jesus talk into one's otherwise normal workaday contacts with the world.

We have said that everybody worships and that worship systems are just one part of the total picture. So with witness. Everyone witnesses, whatever they may be doing. We have also said that the whole world is at worship and is in some way witnessing about who or what it worships. This is another way of saying that witness is overheard worship. Witness can take place systematically as a specialty, or it may take place serendipitously, appearing naturally and in any number of forms among the usual habits of our workaday lives. The specialists are usually called evangelists; the serendipitous are those whose worship is so ardent that they are prepared at any time or in any place to speak on behalf of the one they worship.

While the call to specialized witness may come to a few, serendipitous witness is everybody's responsibility. If ignored, only one conclusion can be drawn: there is little or no commitment to the object of their worship.

As music making for Christians is first and foremost an act of worship, music participates in witness as a part of overheard worship. One of the amazing aspects of truth is that all of it is gospel. This is what the apostle Paul was talking about in 1 Corinthians 14:22–25. If an unbeliever happens in on a meeting of Christians and they are prophesying (instead of speaking in tongues), Paul's contention is that this very act of speaking truth to each other will lead an unbeliever to be "convicted by all . . . called to account by all." According to verse 25, the secrets of the visitor's heart will be disclosed, and ". . . he will fall on his face and worship God, declaring that God is certainly among you" (NASB).

This being said, we should not be content with the idea that overheard worship and worship music are all we need. There is also a very necessary and worthwhile body of music and musicians designed and called specifically to convey the importance, the need, and the way of becoming a new creature. The gospel must be sung, not just preached. This means that some people will be called to sing the gospel. They bear heavy responsibility to sing well, clearly, uncompromisingly, simply, and humbly.

Even so, witnessing with music is not without its detractors. Some people's musical preferences do not include the styles so often employed by musical witnesses, and others, for well-considered philosophical reasons, find problems in witness art. We shall pass over the first type here because we have already devoted considerable time to the defense of pluralism and to criticizing those who are bound to a narrow spectrum of musical practice. Instead, we shall spend some time on the problems inherent in direct musical witness, for there are some very real ones. But first we will outline some of the more positive aspects of witness music.

Values of Witness Music

Witness music is effective. It works. People are moved to repentance and drawn to Christ. And why not? If the gospel is the power of God unto salvation and if the gospel is sung, it follows that the power of God will be made manifest in the midst of its singing. It cannot be said any more simply than that. Detractors will say that its effectiveness is due more to the emotional content brought about by the combined force of singer and song or due to the force of familiar, perhaps sentimental, melodies and harmonies. While this may be the case, and while the misuse of music will always be a problem, no one should really be all that upset over the emotional appeal of simple messages simply sung. In saying this, we should differentiate between expressive singing and manipulation. But this is not a problem reserved just for singers of the gospel. It is for every Christian who makes music for any reason.

Many singers of the gospel are humble, dedicated, and called people. They are trustworthy and whole. Many of them are sensitive musicians, possessed of a keen appreciation for the larger world of excellence, who have laid some or all of it aside in order to work at the level to which God has called them. Others are not very musically sensitive. There are holes in their musicianship and aesthetic sensitivities. But integrity and humility compensate, and in the midst of weakness the strength of God is made perfect. These people are different from the hucksters—some of them extremely gifted—who admittedly make a shambles of witness music, singing it not so much because they love Jesus and want to bring others to the same love, but simply because they're good, they know it, they take advantage of it, and they have found this medium to be quite lucrative.

Witness music keeps the church from the temptation of making music solely for itself in the exclusivity of corporate worship. While we have already argued that worship without witness is not true worship, it is very easy to forget this and turn the gathering of the family of God into a closed circle, forgetting what it means and possibly costs to sing to sinners. We can easily perpetuate the error that there is church music and gospel music, not just divided into different musical types and styles, but different philosophies, one for worship and one for persuasion. This is wrong. The church, in its multiple activities, is one; its worship, in its many manifestations, is one; and its musics, in all of their varieties, are one.

Witness music keeps forcing the issue of musical and textual candor, simplicity, and plainspokenness. When done biblically, it follows Jesus' kind of plainspokenness. While befriending sinners, he did not hesitate to be blunt with them and make them think. He forced people to decide between nonbelief and unbelief. That is, because of the very nature of this mysteriously simple gospel, some turned away never to follow him again. Others, puzzled but hungry, believing but unbelieving, kept coming back for more of this simple straightforward stuff. Good witness music seeks to tell the whole truth, just as good worship music does. Each kind of music should confirm and dislodge at the same time.

Witness music puts the church on its mettle, not just to make good music, but to show that it has reasons for making music that lie beyond the purely aesthetic. This makes all of the church's music accountable as witness music, not just as good music. While the world might simply make good music, the church rises above this and makes good music for the glory of God, for the edification of those who are right side up, and for the re-creation of those who are upside down.

Witness music rests in the power of God, just as worship music does. While each body of music has its own legitimate but limited force, neither can claim to act on its own simply because the force is there. Good witness music somehow eventually must disappear in order to make God all in all. The same is true of worship music. Each kind must play a role similar to that of the Holy Spirit, one of whose purposes is to make Christ real rather than to be the center of attention. Witness music has value only as it decreases in order that Christ may increase.

Problems in Witness Music

While witness music has many things to commend it, some problems should be noted.

Witness music can easily become Christians' pacifier music or Muzak. While Christians should be going on to deeper musical things, some keep hanging on, repeating the familiar, and delighting in emotional memories that they should have long since replaced. Also, because the most effective witness music is texted music, and because it may have been effective in bringing someone to Christ, the assumption may be perpetuated that only texted music can bring spiritual pleasure or nurture to the Christian. To use an analogy from Scripture, some Christians remain content with milk music instead of going for meat music.

Witness music can be misused as a soft-sell "come-on" to a hard-sell evangelistic message. The soft-sell/hard-sell combination, so typical to commerce, is out of place in evangelism. When witness music is used primarily to soften people's emotions instead of to sing the truth; when the evangelistic message is designed to exploit this softening instead of telling good news; and when, following the message, music is allowed to continue the exploitation in order to bring people to a decision, the gospel is reduced to the level of horse trading and political chicanery. This sullies the name and purpose of authentic evangelists and musical witnesses. Sincere Christians, while frustrated and embarrassed, also wonder why many decisions for Christ don't last very long or why new Christians seem to be so slow in growing up into Christ.

Witness music often gets too far out in front of the gospel. Musical witnesses may be easily tempted to let their music making run out ahead of God, as if the gospel needed the power of music and art to make it manifest. Current evangelical conservatism works on a curious mixture of theologies. On the one hand there is "content" theology, the doctrinal stuff we learn and learn to preach from. It is often heavily tipped toward the sovereignty of God and God's unquestionable control over the affairs of the world. On the other hand, we have "process" theology, the stuff we use to "get spiritual things done," the stuff we worship, evangelize, and persuade with. It leans more toward persuading people whose wills can be bent in the direction of our persuasion. Since we are a nation of persuaders and sellers, free to motivate others and to use techniques that motivate, we may choose an evangelistic approach that fits these national ways. The trouble arises when these national ways become a power, first unto themselves, and only then to salvation.

Witness music, manipulatively used and running out ahead of God, can backfire once people who have been manipulated that way come to God. These newly converted Christians can mistakenly assume that music should always be out front leading the parade, even when the parade is the corporate worship of a God whose power can knock down walls without the parade. Musical witnesses must constantly pray that the personal and musical force at their disposal will always be ready to get out of the way of the very gospel they are singing about.

No one can deny that people often turn worshipfully to God because the music has made them tender toward the words or the stylistic force of the singer has made both words and music into a deeply effective force. But once this happens, it becomes the duty of the ministerial leadership to explain the difference between a message delivered with personal power and the superior power of the message, irrespective of the force and gifts of the deliverers. Failure to do this can easily lead to the idolatry of personality cults and musical determinism, in which the singer or the sayer and the style in which the gospel is sung or said become so important that nothing much can be thought to happen without them. The medium becomes the message or, at the very least, inseparable from it.

There is probably too much witness music compared to its effectiveness. Instead of being an integrated part of evangelism, witness music has turned into a separate industry. Its very attractiveness simply as music, as easy listening and entertainment, makes it immensely popular, not because the gospel message is important, but because the music is. And, as mentioned in the first concern, more Christians listen to it than non-Christians. One of the best examples of what can happen is in the field of traditional gospel music. Its best audience draw is in concerts instead of outreach meetings. And one wonders if the same has not begun to happen to Christian contemporary music.

The effectiveness of witness music can mistakenly reinforce the idea that all art can witness the way texted art does. In other words, the power of truth and the force of handiwork can get confused. In the case of witness music, the emotional power of music can make it appear that it is really the text doing all of the work. But what happens when the music is taken away and the text—the truth part—is left to itself? Can we trust its power, or do we need to run interference for it with music?

But even texted art can prove itself to be foolishness when it comes to witness. The danger in much Christian literature and drama is exaggeration, oversimplification, and even naive caricaturing. These art forms often fail the very substance of truth itself by trying to run out ahead of it or help it along or work on its behalf in order to "get to" ordinary people. The result is less than the truth, less than art, and an outright insult to ordinary people. In its very banality, it turns into snobbery, because it looks down on people's— average people's—innate powers of observation and creativity. Christian artists need to remember that great artists, both Christian and non-Christian, understand that naked truth is so powerful that it need not be exaggerated, made overly obvious, or helped along; that it has a unique, self-inhering way of coming at us from any angle and in any number of vocabularies.

Christian drama can deteriorate into costumed preachment and bring the Word down to the level of the average sitcom. The failure of sitcom is the same as the failure of pseudorealism in the visual arts. The "truth" is averaged out, all-inclusive, or exaggerated. "Sitcom" witness, like television sitcoms, superficially looks real, appears to be practical, but isn't. Instead of presenting ideas powerfully, it presents them subrealistically, by exaggerating, oversimplifying, or caricaturing. But power and exaggeration are two entirely different things, just as true reality and superficial reality are. The gospel is power, not exaggeration, true reality, not cartoon reality. Any attempt to reduce it to these is to fail in the task of witness, no matter how much we want to use the arts to get the job done.

As to liturgical dance, unless it is allowed to be itself it can turn into a limited, simplistic, asensual, unbodied activity, in which an otherwise rich repertory of gesture is turned into the adult equivalent of children's motion choruses.

These principles are all the more important on the mission field with Christians who use indigenous art as a "tool for evangelism" among people who have never heard of Christ. The phenomenon of evangelizing ethnomusicologists and ethnoartists and ethnodramatists is relatively new and, in some cases, theologically naive. In many pagan cultures art forms cannot be separated from worldview; they literally *are* "truth," and this makes it all the more tempting and all the more dangerous to couch the Christian message in art forms as a primary means of evangelism. The witness artist must first of all find out to what extent the receiving culture has, in its own worldview, confused its artifacts with its beliefs. If the two are really separate—and the very nature of fallenness works against their being so—then artistic evangelism can possibly be contemplated, assuming that neither truth nor art is blunted in the process.

But if artifacts are not separate from beliefs, then evangelizing with art might simply lead to "christianizing" a false worldview, in which case both the witness and the results are syncretistic—the commingling of two opposing worldviews. The next step is obvious. Syncretistic evangelism means syncretistic worship. And bringing this back to American culture, with its obsession with pragmatism and commercialism, syncretism may easily take the form of gospel as manipulation, which in turn leads to worship as manipulation.

There is little evidence anywhere in Scripture about witnessing directly with *music or art.* In both the Old Testament and the New Testament, the primary direction of music is toward God. This lack of evidence about witness art and music should not necessarily be taken as a sign that it should be prohibited. Instead, we can assume that if the Scriptures do not specifically prohibit something, it may be practiced.

But in the New Testament in particular, where the spread of the gospel was the ultimate inevitability of God's redemptive love in Christ, we find a noticeable silence about the use of music in any context other than Christian fellowship.

There are three possible reasons for this silence. First, music created specifically for witness may have actually been used but was not recorded in the New Testament as a separate or significant action. This seems unlikely, in that the narrative portions of the Acts of the Apostles and those less frequently found in the epistles are quite detailed as to what the church undertook in its witness.

Second, the best, most direct witness is word and deed. This being true, music may have been kept out of direct acts of witness because the very urgency of spreading the gospel as quickly and accurately as possible, from evangelist to hearers as well as from person to person, precluded the use of music. That is, even at its simplest and most direct, good art and music are not all that efficient when it comes right down to the urgent necessity to speak truth clearly and unequivocally.

The third possible reason deals with the relationship of Christian to non-Christian perceptions as to the meaning and role of music. The cultural contexts of the early church comprised a mixture of Greek and Roman thought. This was also a world in which the arts were richly and variously at work. It was likewise a world in which clear philosophical views were held as to the moral qualities that the arts and music were believed to possess. Musical types, based on individual scale systems or modes, were believed to induce specific behaviors in the participants, running the gamut from morality to immorality. Although articulated in a very sophisticated way by the Greeks, the ethical doctrines in the arts was part of a deep flaw in their worldview.

It is difficult to conceive of the apostles, especially Paul, being ignorant of this thought system. Assuming them to know what was going on in the secular world, and assuming them to enjoy music making themselves, we can guess that they entertained one of at least three strategies concerning the use of music in witness. They could have considered adopting or christianizing the prevalent thought system and choosing a musical style that was already perceived by general culture to be conducive to upright behavior, coupling it to Christian words, and waiting for the desired effect.

Or, sensing that doing this would be syncretistic or that another "meat offered to idols" issue would be raised, they postponed using music until the church could handle the entire issue biblically within its corporate practices.

Or perhaps the apostles simply believed that the young church should not express itself musically to the outside world until it possessed an authentic music of its own, one that bore no associative relevance to that of general culture. By instructing itself in psalms, hymns, and spiritual songs, the young church would gradually build up an authentic repertoire of musical practice, both out of its Jewish traditions and the uniquely new songs coming directly from this new faith. Eventually this new music could be used as witness music, not so much to sound like the music of the culture to which the witness was directed, but to demonstrate that the entirety of the Christian life generated an entirety of Christian practice of which the rest of the world could then take clear notice.

Our secularized culture is bound by one of the same flaws that bound Greco-Roman thought. Handiwork is given a power that it does not intrinsically possess. Music is used as a tool, as a behavioral agent, and people willingly submit themselves to it instead of assuming themselves to be masters of it. Consequently, music is both praised and blamed for what it is allegedly capable of doing to people. The church, having been diluted early on in its history both by systematic and unsystematic Platonism, has yet to articulate a fully biblical perspective on the way the power and beauty of music should be constantly subject to the sovereignty of its users, who are in turn subject to the sovereignty of their Creator.

Until this happens, it would be well for evangelistic leadership to consider these issues, to back away from its heavy, sometimes intemperate, dependence on music as a tool for evangelism, and to depend more directly on the inestimable power of Word and deed, lived and preached powerfully, unequivocally, and humbly. In other words, the very strength of the gospel could well make the abundance of witness art into foolishness, not God's but ours.

To summarize, Christians who make art have two tasks. The first is to make excellent art, which might or might not directly witness. Whether it does or doesn't, its first task is to be excellent art, appropriately chosen and creatively diverse, the content and quality of which should parallel the excellence of the gospel itself. The second task is to understand that Christian artists are witnesses, whatever they do. The lives they lead are primarily as living epistles and secondarily as artistic witnesses. Even those whose art is word and deed art—literature, drama, film, video, and to a certain extent witness music and dance—cannot assume that their art fulfills their witness quota. Their art is their work, the same way a computer specialist has his or her work. Meantime, they are to proclaim the gospel directly, with every breath, in any situation, and with every act.

Musical Meaning, the New Creation, and Musical Indigeneity

Our discussion now comes full circle. The debate that Christians have traditionally had with artistic content has either been over new and disturbing art or the borrowing and adapting of art with forbidden associations. The first issue has little importance because of the church's failure of late to show itself to be a new creation by being newly creative. The church has gradually become a haven for musical repetition, familiarity, and borrowing. The relationship of faith to newness has been largely overlooked in favor of faith—if it can be called that—as repetition and addiction to the familiar. There seems to be an all-too-prevalent fear among pastors, evangelists, and strategists of renewal that non-Christian people might be turned away by artistic originality, stylistic variety, or, for that matter, truly prophetic preaching.

Another reason why the church overborrows stems from a misinterpretation of Jesus' strategy of speaking in the language of the people. While some Christians may assume that simple witness means simple art, and simple means quickness, immediacy, or the lowest common perceptual denominator, Jesus depended solely on the straightforward bluntness and immeasurable force of truth. While church growth strategists may assume that speaking in the language of the people is the best way to get a message across in the shortest possible time with the least amount of conceptual dissonance, Jesus spoke "simply" in such a way as to lead to his crucifixion. But the more carefully we read the gospels, the more we come away with the conviction that some of Jesus' thinnest milk was stronger than much of our contemporary meat. And assuming, for the sake of argument, that prevailing strategies are ideal for winning souls, should we assume that they should be carried over into leading the body of Christ into maturity?

In any case, it has turned out that many evangelists and church growth leaders scout out culture, identifying what works, borrowing this, imitating that, and, in the process, dragging in numerous artistic and musical associations from the very culture that they then turn around and condemn in their preaching. In the name of being a radically recreated and new creation, supposedly capable of radically new and different things, the church mimics and clones, hoping to win a world that, in its own creative ways, sets the tone for what the church turns around and claims to be its song. All the while, many think themselves to be doing God a great service by being courageous enough to break so-called traditional molds, divesting themselves of the "old ways," only to launch out into a vocabulary of imitation.

This is a fact: *Somebody will always be creatively authentic.* So why shouldn't it be the church? If it is true that the gospel is foolishness to those seeking wisdom and a scandal to those seeking signs (1 Corinthians 1:23); if it is true that new creatures make new things, not only because they are enabled to, but because they are commanded to (Psalm 33:3); if it is true that those who live by faith are the most capable of receiving, celebrating, and offering up the newest, the most daring, and—in the biblical sense—the most scandalous; then is it not something approaching outright shame for the church to be content with artistic inauthenticity and creative secondhandedness? What drives its strategies? Is it fear of small results, fear of not communicating, not pleasing, not meeting people's "felt needs," not helping God out enough? Will God panic and lose the world if we make music and art that might turn out to have the ring of authenticity to it?

Now let's return to the principle of associative meaning discussed in chapter 2 because, strangely enough, this is where the secret lies for authentically created worship and witness music. All along we have been arguing that music has no intrinsically sacred meaning or secular meaning. We have argued instead that its meaning is brought about by repeated use in a given context, which then "imputes" meaning that music does not intrinsically possess.

Because it is true that music quickly absorbs meaning from its immediate surroundings, this principle should work just as effectively when music, born first in the church, develops its primary associations there. Then if any perceptual dissonance takes place, it will take place in culture *as a result of what the church does, not the reverse.* And why not? Why not let the best and newest creativity happen first in the church, where the associations and associative meanings are first of all holy, winsome, and of good report? Why not assume that the church is capable of getting the associative jump on culture?

This is what biblically based indigeneity is: new songs in the church, the best songs in the church *first.* That is not beauty equaling truth or art equaling holiness, but artistic creativity found in primary *contextual* relationship to these attributes. This is artistic creativity reminding humankind that the Christian imagination is not satisfied with stasis or mimicry. This is Christian creativity understanding that to be created in God's image and then recreated to conform to it mean accepting the continual responsibility of firstness. And new art always brings firstness and disturbance just as the new birth does. It does not always have to be thundering and unrelenting. It can be just as apparent in meek and humble song. Whatever its volume, length, or magnitude, new art brings freshness and dislodgment.

In its own way music is prophecy, prophecy toward new birth and toward reformation. The Christian community cannot be just a community of new hearts and minds in the abstract, but a working outreach of new creativity. The communion of saints is not just a mystical and spiritual oneness. It is also an active, aggressive, faithful, sojourning, and relational communion. It is trusting and unsuspicious communion, unlike those in which artistic and musical newness cause discomfort and mistrust. And it is a communion that thrusts its newness out into the world, content to let the chips fall, not where they may, but where the Holy Spirit lodges them.

This is artistic and musical indigeneity. This is the church in its many-tongued creativities constantly showing its authenticity—quite unlike anyone else. It is from within the church that word and deed disturb and transform culture, while art pieces befriend these actions.

Then if borrowing is going to take place, let the world borrow from the church. If artistic leadership is part of artistic creativity, then let the people of the church reestablish artistic leadership. Or let the world ignore it all, if it so chooses. But let the church understand, with the clearest of consciences, that it can do much better than it has done lately, and let the celebration be what the Scriptures describe it to be: a perpetual enthroning of Jahweh upon its praises (Psalm 22:3, NASB), and a proclamation of this to the world. This brings art and music to their full and final meaning. And it changes the debate from one of superficial controversy to the paradox of celebration, scandal, stumbling block, and gospel.

BIBLIOGRAPHY

Balliett, Whitney. *American Musicians: Fifty Six Portraits in Jazz*. New York: Oxford University Press, 1986.

Best, Harold M. "The Art of New Music." *Contemporary Christian Magazine* (March 1984): 10–11.

_____. "Music Curricula in the Future." *Arts Policy Review* (November-December, 1992): 2–7

Blamires, Harry. *The Christian Mind*. Ann Arbor: Servant Books, 1978.

Brantlinger, Patrick. *Bread & Circuses: Theories of Mass Culture as Social Decay*. Ithaca: Cornell University Press, 1983.

Cage, John. *Silence*. Middletown: Wesleyan University Press, 1961.

Chenoweth, Vida. *Melodic Perception and Analysis*. Ukurumpa, E.H.D., Papua New Guinea: Summer Institute of Linguistics, 1972.

Copland, Aaron. *What to Listen for in Music*. New York: McGraw-Hill, 1957.

David, Hans T. and Arthur Mendel, eds. *The Bach Reader*. rev. ed. New York: W. W. Norton & Company, 1966.

DeMol, Karen. "On Musical Excellence." *Pro Rege* (Vol. XX, No. 4, June 1992): 1–10.

Elliott, David J. "Key Concepts in Multicultural Education." *International Journal of Music Education* (No. 13, 1989): 11–18.

Eskew, Harry and Hugh T. McElroth. *Sing With Understanding: An Introduction to Christian Hymnody*. Nashville: Broadman, 1991.

Evans, David. *Big Road Blues*. Berkeley: University of California Press, 1982.

Frith, Simon, ed. *Facing the Music*. New York: Pantheon Books, 1988.

Green, Barry. *The Inner Game of Music*. Garden City: Anchor Press/Doubleday, 1986.

Gridley, Mark C. *Jazz Styles*. Englewood Cliffs: Prentice-Hall, 1978.

Grout, Donald Jay. *A History of Western Music*. 3rd ed. with Claude V. Palisca, New York: W. W. Norton & Company, 1980.

Harris, Michael W. *Thomas A. Dorsey and the Rise of Gospel Blues*. New York: Oxford University Press, 1991.

Heilbut, Anthony. *The Gospel Sound*. New York: Limelight Editions, 1985.

Hood, Mantle. *The Ethnomusicologist*. New York: McGraw-Hill, 1971.

Hustad, Donald. *Jubilate! Church Music in the Evangelical Tradition*. Carol Stream: Hope Publishing Company, 1981.

Jackson, Irene V., ed. *More Than Dancing*. Westport: Greenwood Press, 1985.

Kivy, Peter. *Sound and Semblance: Reflections on Musical Representation*. Princeton: Princeton University Press, 1984.

Lehrdal, Fred and Ray Jackendoff. *A Generative Theory of Tonal Music*. Cambridge: MIT Press, 1983.

L'Engle, Madeleine. *Walking on Water*. Wheaton: Harold Shaw, 1980.

Leonard, Neil. *Jazz: Myth and Religion*. New York: Oxford University Press, 1987.

Lockerbie, Bruce. *The Timeless Moment*. Westchester: Crossway Books, 1980.

Manoff, Tom. *Music: A Living Language*. New York: W. W. Norton & Company, 1982.

Manuel, Peter. *Popular Musics of the Non-Western World: An Introductory Survey*. Oxford: Oxford University Press, 1988.

Meyer, Leonard B. *Music, The Arts and Ideas*. Chicago: The University of Chicago Press, 1967.

————. *Emotion and Meaning in Music*. Chicago: The University of Chicago Press, 1956.

Myers, Kenneth A. *All God's Children and Blue Suede Shoes*. Westchester: Crossway Books, 1989.

Morgan, Robert P. *Twentieth Century Music*. New York: W. W. Norton & Company, 1991.

Nettl, Bruno. *The Study of Ethnomusicology*. Urbana: University of Illinois Press, 1983.

————. *Theory and Method in Ethnomusicology*. London: The Free Press of Glencoe, 1964.

————. *The Western Impact on World Music*. New York: Schirmer Books, 1985.

Ouelette, Don. "An Interview with Sam Phillips." *The Other Side* (May-June, 1990): 54–57.

Pass, David B. *Music and the Church*. Nashville: Broadman, 1989.

Pleasants, Henry. *The Agony of Modern Music*. New York: Simon & Schuster, 1955.

————. *The Great American Popular Singers*. New York: Simon & Schuster, 1974.

Ravitch, Diane. "Multiculturalism." *The American Scholar* (Summer 1990): 337–354.

Reynolds, Simon. *Blissed Out: The Raptures of Rock*. London: Serpent's Tail Books, 1990.

Rochberg, George. *The Aesthetics of Survival: A Composer's View of Twentieth Century Music*. Ann Arbor: The University of Michigan Press, 1984.

Rockwell, John. *All American Music: Composition in the Late Twentieth Century*. New York: Vintage Press, 1984.

Routley, Eric. *Church Music and the Christian Faith*. Carol Stream: 1978.

Sachs, Curt. *The Wellsprings of Music*. Reprint. New York: DaCapo Press, 1962.

Sayers, Dorothy. *The Mind of The Maker*. San Francisco: Harper & Row, 1987.

Schaeffer, John. *New Sounds: A Listener's Guide to New Music*. New York: Harper & Row, 1987.

Schultze, Quentin, Roy M. Anker, James D. Bratt, William D. Romanowski, John William Worst, and Lambert Zuidervaart. *Dancing in the Dark*. Grand Rapids: William B. Eerdmans, 1991.

Seerveld, Calvin. *Rainbows for a Fallen World*. Toronto: Tuppence Press, 1980.

Sessions, Roger. *The Musical Experience of Composer, Performer, Listener*. Princeton: Princeton University Press, 1987.

Shaw, Arnold. *Black Popular Music in America*. New York: Schirmer Books, 1986.

Spencer, Jon Michel. *Protest and Praise: Sacred Music of Black Religion*. Minneapolis: Fortress Press, 1991.

Stravinsky, Igor. *Poetics of Music in the Form of Six Lessons*. New York: Vintage Books, 1956.

Tirro, Frank. *Jazz: A History*. New York: W. W. Norton & Company, 1977.

Turner, Steve. *Hungry for Heaven: Rock and Roll and the Search for Redemption*. London: Virgin Books, 1988.

Underhill, Evelyn. *Worship*. New York: Crossroad, 1989.

Van Olst, E. H. *The Bible and Liturgy*. 3rd ed. Grand Rapids: William B. Eerdmans, 1991.

Ward, Ed. *Rock of Ages: the Rolling Stone History of Rock and Roll*. New York: Rolling Stone Press, 1986.

Webber, Robert E. *Worship Old and New*. Grand Rapids: Zondervan, 1982.

Westermeyer, Paul. *The Church Musician*. San Francisco: Harper & Row, 1988.

White, James F. *Introduction to Christian Worship*. Nashville: Abingdon, 1990.

Wicke, Peter. *Rock Music: Culture, Aesthetics and Sociology*. Cambridge: Cambridge University Press, 1987.

Williams, Martin, ed. *The Art of Jazz*. New York: DaCapo Press, 1980.

Wolfe, Tom. "The Worship of Art." *Harper's* (October, 1984): 61–68.

Wolterstorff, Nicholas. *Art in Action*. Grand Rapids: William B. Eerdmans, 1980.

Zuckerkandl, Victor. *Man the Musician*. Princeton: Princeton University Press, 1973.

INDEX

DATE DUE			
950703			